What Readers are Saying about DISRUPTED

Here's the book I wish I'd had last year when my dad passed away, and I was feeling unmoored and uncertain. It's also the book I need right now as I still try to move forward after the loss of someone so irreplaceable in my life. Jen has the words and guidance we need when we are gripped with sorrow—and needing hope for tomorrow.

—Jennifer Dukes Lee
Author of *Growing Slow* and *Stuff I'd Only Tell God*

This is a beautifully written book. If you, or anyone you know, is looking for a playbook on dealing with terminal illness and grief, you must take this book on your journey. This is a highly relatable book. The author feels like both a friend and coach. As a clinical psychologist, *Disrupted* has my highest endorsement.

—Barbara Greenberg, PhD

This book may have been written for children whose parents are facing a terminal illness, but it will serve anyone who is walking through a terminal illness with someone they love. In my case, my sister, who was diagnosed with a fast-growing and aggressive brain tumor. When your world has been shattered by the news of a bleak and certain diagnosis, it helps to have someone in your life who understands. Not just someone who has walked in your shoes, but someone who has lived in your skin. Though our stories are very different, Jen and the others who shared their personal experiences in this book understand. They offer empathy and insight without trying to fix a thing. And, maybe just as important and helpful, you'll find permission to grieve and hope and live within the context of heartache and, at times, debilitating anguish. Often, we wonder how to love and care for friends and family beyond a home-cooked meal and constant prayer. In *Disrupted*, I now have a gift that will make a difference.

—Robin Dance
Life Plan Advisor and Author of
For All Who Wander and *The Journey Guide*

With the voice of a wise mentor and the comfort of your closest friend, Jen has used her own experience and expertise to give us this incredibly important resource. If you should find yourself in this painfully nuanced position of grief, I'm so sorry. I know you'll be comforted and helped by Jen's words in *Disrupted*.

—Nicole Zasowski
Marriage and Family Therapist and Author of
What If It's Wonderful?

We all know death is part of life. But when death is breathing down a parent's neck or comes like an unexpected thief in the night, few of us know what to expect, how to process our grief, or what it looks like to move forward with the constant companion of a loss we'll never "get over." Here's the good news: you don't have to navigate this alone. Jen Babakhan is the trustworthy voice of a friend and grief mentor you need. If you have a parent with a terminal illness, or know someone who does, don't delay in getting a copy of *Disrupted*. You will be grateful you did.

—Becky Keife
Author of *The Simple Difference* and
Create in Me a Heart of Peace

DISRUPTED

FINDING PEACE WITH A PARENT'S TERMINAL ILLNESS

Jen Babakhan

Disrupted: Finding Peace with a Parent's Terminal Illness
Copyright © 2023, 2025 by Jen Babakhan

Published in association with Story Architect. www.booksandsuch.com

All rights reserved. No part of this publication may be reproduced, stored in a retrieval system, or transmitted in any form or by any means—electronic, mechanical, photocopy, recording or any other—except for brief quotations in printed reviews without the written prior permission of the publisher.

No AI Training. Any use of this publication to "train" artificial intelligence (AI) technologies to generate text is expressly prohibited.

Unless otherwise noted, Scripture quotations marked (NIV) are taken from the Holy Bible, New International Version®, NIV®. Copyright © 1973, 1978, 1984, 2011 by Biblica, Inc.® Used by permission of Zondervan. All rights reserved worldwide. www.zondervan.com The "NIV" and "New International Version" are trademarks registered in the United States Patent and Trademark Office by Biblica, Inc.®

Cover Design by Barefaced Creative Media

Print ISBN: 978-1-962845-15-1

Printed in the United States of America

FOR MOM, DAD, AND ZACH

Mom—*I kept writing. This is for you. Meet you at the gates.*
Dad—*You've taught me how to love well in the face of loss and beyond. I'm forever grateful.*
Zach—*You kept me grounded and never hesitated to stand beside me during the really hard stuff. You're the kind of brother everyone should have.*

TABLE OF CONTENTS

Introduction · IX

Chapter One: An Earthquake for One: Enduring the
  Moments That Shake Your Soul· 1
Chapter Two: Fumbling Through Fog: Doing What's
  Needed When You Want Normal Back· · · · · · · · · · · · · · · · · 11
Chapter Three: The Murky Middle: The Emotional
  Rollercoaster of Care and Arrangements· · · · · · · · · · · · · · · · 23
Chapter Four: The Lasts and Firsts: Holding Hope in
  Uncertainty and Sorrow· 40
Chapter Five: Anticipating the Impossible: Loving Yourself by
  Preparing For Future Grief · 52
Chapter Six: Say All The Things: Finding Peace in the
  Before and After · 63
Chapter Seven: Keep Some Air for Yourself: Why Saving
  Room for Normal is Non-negotiable · · · · · · · · · · · · · · · · · · 74
Chapter Eight: The Eye of the Storm: Witnessing the Worst
  and Processing the Surreal Reality of Death · · · · · · · · · · · · · · 85
Chapter Nine: Walking Through Broken Glass:
  Your New Life, Grief, and Family Roles· · · · · · · · · · · · · · · · 106
Chapter Ten: Resilient Hope: Embracing the Finality of
  Death with Peace ·121

Closing Thoughts ·135
Notes ·137
Acknowledgments· ·139

INTRODUCTION

It's not often an author begins a book by saying they're sorry. I may be the first—but I *am* sorry. I'm sorry that you have any need for this book. I really wish you didn't.

I hate that any of us have a need for a book about finding a way through the illness and nearing death of a parent. Death feels wrong, like a glitch in this whole system, because it is. Life was never meant to be this way. And yet here we are, stuck between now and the not yet of God's redemptive plan, feeling the implications of that ugly glitch more than we dreamed possible.

Life before the word *terminal* feels like a distant place. I know. It's full of comforting and carefree memories and yet a painful reminder of how much has changed—how much has already been lost. Chances are, before, you were quick to offer sympathy to others experiencing life-altering news or even donate to a fundraiser to help in a tangible way. But then got on with your day. You went to work or stayed home with your kids. You sat in meetings and traffic. You shopped for work pants that were never stretchy enough for your liking. You took calls and filled your kids' water bottles, unloaded the dishwasher for the umpteenth time, and the most pressing thing you had on your mind was trying to remember to bring your grocery list with you to the store.

In the beginning, after you get *the news*, the fog clouding your daily life is thick. It's difficult to muster up the strength to care about the minor things your friends complain about. They still live in luxurious oblivion—where you once were. It feels lonely in this new place of tender existence. Hearing that your mother or father— the very foundation of your life's story—has a shortened time left on earth has a way of muting the noise of the world.

On one hand, it's hard to comprehend this truth on the most basic level. Our parents have always been here, how will he or she... *not* be here? On the other, death is a certainty for all of us, and we've most likely assumed we would outlive our parents—so why is it so shocking when you hear there's a time frame for it? When your parent is given a set amount of weeks, months, or even years to live—how do you not try to live them all at once? To squeeze in every memory you planned to have over the next three decades into a year? Six months?

Every family is unique, and therefore every experience is unique. After all, no one has *your* mother or father. No one can truly be with you in the way you desperately ache for them to be. Hear me now—that feeling—the one that sits heavy on your chest and threatens to stop your breathing entirely, is lying to you. Never think you are alone in this. Others *do* understand.

You may not know anyone personally who has experienced the terminal diagnosis of someone close, much less a parent, but those of us who *have* are out there—and in this book. Throughout these pages, you will find the experiences of other women who have walked where you are walking now. These women have lost a beloved parent to a terminal illness in various stages of life. Their stories are different, but one thread remains consistent throughout each: they know this pain too.

I'm honored to introduce you to the women whose experiences, sprinkled through each chapter along with my own, will blanket you in understanding and empathy. You will meet:

- Quantrilla Ard, PhD, grief and loss coach, lost her mother when she was twenty-two years old to sarcoidosis and a fungal infection. Her mother, Quantrilla Edwards Carter, was forty-four.
- Mary Boswell, women's ministry leader, whose mother passed of pancreatic cancer when Mary was forty-seven. Her mother, Ann Story, was seventy-four.
- Sophie Hudson, author, speaker, and podcast host, whose mother had dementia and passed when Sophie was forty-six. Her mother, Ouida, was eighty-four.

- Becky Keife, author, lost her father to congestive heart failure when she was twenty-eight. Her father, Ralph, was fifty-nine.
- Shay Mason, author, whose father died of pancreatic cancer when she was forty-eight. Her father, John, was seventy-four.
- Becky McCoy, writer and podcast host, lost her father to liposarcoma, a rare cancer, when she was twenty-six. Her father, Mike, was fifty-two.
- Jaime Jo Wright, author, whose mother passed away from a rare form of stomach cancer when Jaime was forty-five. Her mother, Joann, was seventy-five.

Each of their experiences hold poignant moments, hard-earned wisdom, and undeniable truths. I know you will find empathy and understanding in each of them.

When my mother, Carrie, was diagnosed with terminal cancer at sixty-three, and told, in error, she had weeks to live, I was blessed to have one friend—a new one, at that— who had traveled this ever-changing and soul-shifting road ahead of me. My friend told me she would tell me as much as I wanted to know about cancer and the dying process.

I didn't want to know much. Mom's diagnosis was hours old, and I was terrified of every minute that ticked past. The more time that passed, the closer I got to her death. How was I going to survive anything that was coming? I wanted time to stop. Or rewind. Anything to go back to the day before it all changed forever.

In between begging God to save her and change the reality I was living, I raged against Him. How could He allow this to happen? Certainly this was not His plan for my family. Yet it was.

My hope is this book will be the friend who has been there, walking next to you—encouraging you, inspiring you, and proving to you that you can and will survive the days to come. You may not know anyone who has been through this. So, let this book be that friend to you. The voices in this book surround you in spirit, our words forming a tight circle around your pain. We are here. We understand. We stand with you. Let's find hope together.

JEN BABAKHAN

How to Use This Book on Your Journey

I've formatted this book to be both chronological in the experience of having a parent with terminal illness, as well as topical. You may find it helpful to read the chapters in order or jump into the book wherever you are along the journey. Each chapter ends with an "A Moment for Mindfulness" segment that I have included advice from a mental health professional relating to the chapter topic. I highly recommend and value therapy, however, I understand that not everyone has the time and ability to access it, especially in this situation.

I've written this book with the assumption that you have another living parent who may or may not be involved in the caretaking of the ill parent. If you are the sole caretaker of your parent for any reason, I hope you will find ways and other people to lighten your load on this journey as I have suggested throughout the chapters. You have my utmost respect as you love your parent well through such a difficult time.

My deepest hope and prayer is that you find this book useful, in whatever way you choose to read it.

ONE

AN EARTHQUAKE FOR ONE: ENDURING THE MOMENTS THAT SHAKE YOUR SOUL

> They will have no fear of bad news; Their hearts are steadfast, trusting in the Lord.
>
> Psalm 112:7

The call that changed everything came early one Friday in May, the beginning of Mother's Day weekend. I heard my father's gravelly voice on the other end of the phone at seven in the morning, my eyes blurry from sleep. "They think they found cancer in Mom's liver and lungs."

My small sons lay in the bed still peacefully sleeping, their cheeks pink and warm. I saw that I missed his call at five that morning—an alarming fact considering my father rarely called me on the phone—that was something Mom did. "You mean, your mom? Grandma?" I asked, growing more confused.

"No. Your mom," he said grimly. I felt my stomach drop and my legs begin to tingle. "We're at the hospital. We came last night because her blood pressure was high, and they ran some tests."

I heard his words, his usual calm demeanor trying to keep me grounded. It was useless. My head raced, and my heart pounded in my chest. "I'll be right there. Let me call Ed to come home."

My husband Ed had just left for work an hour away. As soon as he answered, the words left my lips in a steady string of panic. "They think Mom has cancer and I need you to come home. Now."

We had lost my father-in-law to cancer the year before. My own father had a diagnosis of prostate cancer the year prior, but was in remission. It felt like we could not catch a break.

His voice was filled with disbelief when he said, "What? Are you sure? I can't believe this. I'll turn around."

Surely, this could not be happening. Again. I don't remember much about the drive to the hospital. I drove with the hum of panic and prayers filling my mind. I turned on the stereo if only to have respite from the noise of my thoughts. The Christian worship music felt cold, as if the singers had never felt pain. They sang of God's faithfulness and the words felt hollow. The cars with me on the freeway sped past carelessly. They were on the way to work, as my husband had been—it was a normal day for them. I sighed. Not for me. I'm going to the hospital. I bet no one else on this freeway is going to the hospital.

In the midst of deep shock and pain, it's startlingly easy to assume no one has felt or experienced the same. I knew God was with me, I just wasn't sure how to find the peace He promises to bring to every circumstance.

When I arrived and found her room, Mom somehow looked older. Lying in the bed, her white hair framed a pale face. She offered me a tired smile. "Hey Baby."

I leaned down to hug her across the wires attached to her body. I gave Dad a hug and received all of the details of the night before. I struggled to make sense of them. High blood pressure, an x-ray that looked fine but then a CT scan that did not. Metastasis to her liver, lungs, and bones—stage four.

"Honey, it's everywhere," Mom said softly when I asked about surgery to remove the tumors.

My brother Zach was in college and would arrive later that day. He's ten years younger than I am. I thought about how this would affect his life, just as it was getting started. How it would affect all of us.

Blurred Reality

When the doctor arrived, a young Hispanic woman who, in my opinion, looked like she could have been on *Grey's Anatomy*, I asked for a moment in the hallway. "Can't you do surgery?" I asked, hopeful we could just cut out this new problem and be done.

"It's too extensive. I'm sorry," she said with sterile compassion.

"How much time does she have left? Please—I need to know," I pleaded.

She studied my face, determining if I could handle the truth. "In these kinds of cases, you're looking at six to eight weeks. Maybe a few longer with treatment."

The words hit me like a gust of hot air, stealing my own oxygen. Still, I appreciated her honesty.

The days that followed are a blur. I walked through countless swinging doors, a tear-blurred waxed floor beneath me. The scent of the hospital became instantly nauseating when I returned each day. I hovered in the liminal space between my inner child and adult, unsure of my ability to live without a mother.

I curled into my mother's hospital bed next to her and sobbed until I was breathless. She held me, just as she had when I was a toddler. I cried in elevators while kind strangers and hospital staff looked away so I wouldn't be embarrassed. Those walking through the hospital with blue and pink balloons for new babies felt like the luckiest people in the world. I felt like a walking broken heart, every step more uncertain than the last.

Safe Ground

When your parent is diagnosed with a life-changing illness, it is vital to have a place that feels familiar and yours. Your body needs the rest. It craves the let down from being constantly on guard.

Each night I returned home with swollen eyes and a broken heart, but grateful to be back in what felt like the last safe place on earth—within the four walls of my home. I could still smell the hospital on my clothes, but I was *safe*.

Safe from the constant panic that a doctor would enter the room with a new test result that showed she had even *less* time. Safe from the constant beep of machines announcing low oxygen saturation or an empty IV bag.

At home, I could settle into my worn leather couch, and pretend life was the same. My kids still needed to be fed and bathed, the annoying YouTube child stars on TV still unboxed toys I had no intention of buying. My boys knew their grandmother was sick, and that Mommy had to be gone each day to be with her—something they understood but hated all the same. I hated it for them. For all of us.

Learning that your mother or father will die is not really news. You've known that fact all of your life. It may have been your biggest childhood fear.

For Shay Mason, whose father was a police officer, the fear of losing her father was constantly at the forefront of her young mind. "Growing up, my greatest fear was losing my father, a police officer. I had heard that statistically, Fridays are the most dangerous nights for police officers and that was when my father worked. I spent each Friday night glued to the front window, terrified of seeing someone walking to our front door to deliver bad news. Learning my father had stage four cancer felt a lot like that sense of dread all over again, knowing there was no way to avoid his death this time."

Death is a natural part of living. Learning that death is imminent is another thing all together. Suddenly, time feels like the enemy you cannot see. One month used to be four weeks—enough time to count but not enough to be considered substantial. A month now is four weeks, each holding seven days that contain twenty-four hours. The time remaining is spent striving to carry your mother or father to life's next chapter in God's presence. There is never enough time.

For Jaime Jo Wright, the unexpected stomach cancer diagnosis leading to her mother's death was faster than anyone imagined. "She began having stomach issues and we assumed it was her gallbladder, as did the doctors. She had some tests and the doctors asked her to come in to talk. She called me that night and sounded anxious, which was typical for my mom. When the doctors spoke to her they explained how dire her situation was—she had three months at most, and treatment would only offer one to two more. Three weeks later she was gone."

Mary Boswell's mother, Ann, received her diagnosis gradually. "My mom had been having some issues we assumed were part of some normal medical issues she had been having, but on one visit to my sister, she was very jaundiced and sick. It was obvious things weren't right with her. They found a mass in the emergency room and when they let us know where it was located, my husband and I both knew it wasn't good. He's an anesthetist, and I'm a former critical care nurse and we knew what we were possibly dealing with. Once we got her connected with surgeons and oncologists at home they didn't say it was terminal, but I knew what I knew—it was pancreatic cancer. We just wanted to spend as much time with her as we could after she had the surgery to remove the mass and had treatment."

In my mother's case, the hospital stay that brought a diagnosis was only the beginning. After being discharged from the hospital, my mother needed to meet with an oncologist to learn if any treatment was available. This doctor was more definitive in her prognosis—she assured us we could treat Mom's cancer, a rare cancer of the bile ducts in the liver called cholangiocarcinoma, and it would possibly allow her another one to three years with us, but it was a terminal diagnosis.

Struggling to find the right words to comfort her, I said, "No one knows what time you have left but God, Mom. You could be the miracle—the one case that has remission."

It gave us both some comfort to think about. It didn't matter if it was *likely*. Anything is possible with God. Hope in God's ability to heal is never false hope.

A New Understanding

In those early weeks, my mind continued to spin forward into the future, but found nowhere to land. *Would she be bald at Christmas? How would I explain a bald grandma to my boys? Did my life now revolve around treatment too? Will the side effects kill her before the cancer? Mom never had to worry about her mother dying when I was little.*

A mixture of grief, fear, anger, and resentment took turns coming to the forefront of my heart. I resisted allowing this hateful new guest in our lives called cancer to infiltrate any part of my life it didn't have to. The truth remained, though. Cancer would touch every part of our lives.

My relationship with my mother was complex, as all mother-daughter relationships are. At its core, there was unyielding and relentless love. On the surface, there were often back and forth annoyances that bubbled into disagreement and sometimes distance. In my experience, there's nothing like a terminal diagnosis to help you zero in on the truth of it all: You love your parent with everything you've got, and they love you with all that they are. When life begins to feel like a stopwatch counting to zero, it has a way of rapidly boiling complexity down to simplicity.

In the end, she's your *mom*. He's your *dad*. The disagreements and hurt feelings feel like wasted time when there's so little of it left. It's a heart-wrenching truth to recognize in the middle of it all—it feels like you finally see what's real, and you desperately wish you could have seen it sooner.

Sophie Hudson expressed her own experience with hindsight. "The dynamics of mothers and daughters and family in general, are such that there's a bit of difference between what our families looked like growing up and the families we ourselves are working to create now. I wish I had been more patient with Mama before her diagnosis and asked her more questions. In general, I wish I had been more mindful that my life with her would not last forever, and better at expressing my gratitude for all she did and taught me. I also think that's the universal experience of being a child, for those of us fortunate to have good parents. If she were here now, she would tell me not to worry about it one bit."

In many ways it feels as though God allows the grief inherent in this journey for this purpose alone—that we might finally see what matters most. That feels both loving and painful to consider, that a loving God would allow for such pain. And yet, there is a very acute understanding of your love for a parent and theirs for you that may not ever become evident without it. God did not cause my mother's cancer, or your parent's illness—but He *will* bring something of value from it.

A Word on Complex and Difficult Relationships

It's worth mentioning here that for some, a terminal diagnosis doesn't bring a realization of lost time and wrongs instantly forgiven. For some, the diagnosis brings more anger for hurts or abuse that never should have occurred—painful experiences you have endured that break the heart of God. It is valid and worthwhile to grieve what you wished had been as well as what was. Your strained or fractured relationship with your parent may not mend overnight, but it is worth a prayer that God would bring healing to your heart regardless of where things stand. He is still in the business of healing and bringing life from death.

Absorbing the Shock

If you walked these early days of flattened-out grief and swollen eyes that won't sleep, it feels anything but normal. However, it *is* completely normal. A friend called me to check in over those first days when my world felt as though it had crumbled around me.

"I'm not sleeping at all. I can't eat," I said.

She responded with the reality I had not considered. "It sounds like you're in shock."

That made so much sense, and in my sleep deprived state, I hadn't considered that my body was in shock. I knew I *felt* shocked. The thought that my body was responding as well brought me an odd sense of relief and comfort.

The news of the previous week sent my entire family into a liminal space. We could not go back to the days before we heard the diagnosis. How I *longed* with every fiber of my being to be back in those days. We weren't yet in a new normal, a place where things felt different but safe. Each day felt as if we hovered in this unsettled space of just existing. I hated every second of it.

Family members came to visit us, and I tried to hide my grief for their sake. It never worked. Laughter felt forced and like a denial of reality. *My mother is dying. Your life is still normal. Ours are never going to be the same again.* My thoughts kept me from hearing much of the light chatter that peppered the visits. Seeing my uncles and aunts circle my mother's bed in tears only made the situation real. We were *that* family now—the one everyone else grieves for.

I sensed I needed to focus on what we did have instead of what we were about to lose. I could either allow myself to mourn the death I knew was coming or focus on the life she was still very much living. The choice to do so was a daily choice, sometimes hourly.

Life often combines joy and sorrow into the same breath. Becky McCoy's father was diagnosed with a rare cancer while she was preparing to welcome her first child with her husband, who was in cancer remission himself.

"My father had been trying to lose weight, and he was, everywhere but his stomach. That was the first sign that tipped my mom off. My husband, Keith, and I were living in Las Vegas at the time. We took my parents, who were visiting from Connecticut, on a hike in Zion National Park. Dad barely made it a fraction of the hike because he had trouble breathing, which was odd for an active guy like him. The doctors found the tumor in his stomach a couple months later, but when they went to remove it they realized it was much more involved than the scans showed. It was treatable, but not curable. It was all really hard to process at the time, it felt like it came out of nowhere."

When the freight train of the word 'terminal' speeds through your life, knocking everything you know to be certain to the periphery, it can feel as though nothing will ever be the same again. There is truth in that. Some things won't ever be the same. Your perspective that once focused on the next vacation or which brand of shoe to buy your kids, is now tipped on its side. The fragility of life is now a neon sign, blinking behind every thought: Life is short. Any of us can die at any time.

There's an upside to this and, of course, a downside. The new perspective allows for a determined commitment to staying in the moment. All we *really* have is now. If we allow ourselves to dive into this thought process headfirst, what was once comforting can become anxiety producing. Living in the moment easily becomes a reason to hold a death grip (pun intended) on your other family members. Since my mother's passing, I'm not ashamed to admit that when my father backs his RAV4 out of our driveway, I ask him to drive safely no less than twice, and tell him that I love him at least three times. I worry more about my brother than is probably healthy.

When you know the brevity of life firsthand, it changes you in ways you cannot comprehend. God sees each way your soul has been impacted. He will use these changes to bring things of value into your life, in ways that only He can.

I don't use the word "good" in relation to what will come of this because I know that is a loaded word. You may wonder how can anything good come from such pain. Valuable, meaningful things *will* be brought from this pain. Right now that may be of little comfort—truthfully in this moment, there may be nothing that brings solace. That's okay. Tuck the truth of His faithfulness to you—not just to all of humanity, but to *you* personally—in your pocket. It will be there when you feel ready to embrace and lean on it.

A Moment for Mindfulness

Sometimes the best way to process shocking news, such as the terminal illness of a parent, is to provide your body and mind with a few different ways to find comfort in the chaos. Licensed Marriage and Family Therapist and Author Nicole Zasowski says, "Often times an unanticipated experience and the response depends on the relationship with the parent. A person might not only be grieving the potential loss of a mother or father, but also any unresolved relationship issues that may come up at this time. This is where having life-giving rhythms that care for the heart, mind, and body is key.

"We are reservoirs, not rivers—we cannot give unless we first fill our tank. In moments when we need to slow down and put the oxygen mask on ourselves first, so to speak, we can ask ourselves, 'What would my five senses record right now in this moment? What do I want to remember seeing, hearing, smelling, tasting, and feeling?' When we incorporate rhythmic actions—like making our bed or having the same cup of tea every day while we recite the same prayer—we cue our body to relax and surrender to what is ultimately a loss of control. These small, doable patterns that cue the body are so important during times of shock, anxiety, and stress."

Consider:

- What are some small patterns you can create or continue to cue your body into relaxation and comfort?

A Daughter's Prayer

God, my heart is broken. So many questions are without answers, Father. You know, though. Help me rest in Your knowledge of our situation and not my own. I cannot see a way through this. I am terrified. I feel alone. Please enter into this space with me. Make Your presence known in every way. Please guide my every step. Give me breath when I feel breathless. Steady my shaking steps. Let me know You are here. I know You are, but I don't always feel it. Please help my family. Amen.

TWO

FUMBLING THROUGH FOG: DOING WHAT'S NEEDED WHEN YOU WANT NORMAL BACK

> He will cover you with His feathers, and under His wings you will find refuge; His faithfulness will be your shield and rampart.
>
> Psalm 91:4

My dear friend Barbara, an author and psychologist, with an East Coast sensibility of cutting through to the core of the matter in the kindest way possible, called to check on me between clients. She is the kind of friend everyone should have—intuitive and honest with true kindness shadowing every word she speaks. "It's time to step up to the plate, Darling," she said.

I stood in the hospital breezeway between two wings, staring through floor-length windows that overlooked the café courtyard below. I told her I felt like I didn't want to wake up and remember the truth the next morning—I wanted to stay asleep and unaware. I explained through tears how I hated to wake each morning, that the moment between sleep and consciousness was a gut punch. I was not suicidal—just avoidant.

Step up to the plate.

Those five words shifted something within me. I could not run from reality, even if I wanted to. It was time to step up to the plate. It was time to do what had to be done.

I ended the call and dialed the number of a high school friend who recently suffered the loss of both parents, though I had not spoken to her in twenty years. Somehow, I knew she would understand exactly where I stood, and I felt only the least bit awkward reaching out to her. I knew she had a close family member who ran a highly esteemed local hospice and home health agency. I was stepping up to the plate. On shaking legs, and with a quivering voice, but I was stepping up all the same. "My mom has cancer and she's terminal," I managed to get out before the tears overtook my voice.

She told me she knew the desperate pain, and that she had also somehow made it to the other side of it—to a place where she didn't fall apart on the phone anymore. I was so desperate to get there myself, it helped to know it was possible. She gave me the home health agency information and offered her well-earned wisdom: "It's going to be hard, but you'll get through this. You will find others who can somehow be what you need after she's gone. Friends who will sit with you when you need it, or who will be there when she can't. I know it doesn't feel like it now. You'll get through it, though, I promise."

I ended the call with tearful gratitude and walked back toward the now-familiar swinging doors to my mother's room. I returned to her bedside with new confidence. I let my father know I was taking care of the details of her home care, and it was then I felt it: I was *doing* it. I was surviving. A gentle strength was growing within me. I knew I would crumble again and again over the days ahead, but I also knew I would pull myself back together. It was safe to fall apart. God would not let me stay that way.

The Manna of Suffering

Maybe you're feeling as though you're falling apart more than pulling together. That is valid and expected. The turning point from agony to action is different for everyone. You may vacillate between the two at different times even after your parent is gone. The unfortunate truth is that one doesn't end before the other begins.

Every phone call I made, I repeated the same information: Mom's name, birthdate, and the new language of our painful reality that included the words incurable, terminal, metastatic, cancer, biopsy, samples, and scans. I never wanted to learn this language and I became more fluent with every day that passed.

There was still agony, and it sat in my throat with every word. While "action" typically connotes a swift movement, mine was anything but. Each phone call cost more energy than I felt I had to spend, and I had what I needed. It was the manna of suffering.

Jaime Jo Wright felt as though once her mother received a diagnosis, the wait for the inevitable was unbearable. "I went through a whole barrage of emotions. Some of them, I hated myself for, because there was a part of me that felt like I couldn't live with not knowing when she was going to die. The short time span between diagnosis and her death was probably the best-case scenario for my mom and I both with our anxiety issues. Not knowing and being held in suspense was worse than the actual event for me."

Where is God?

Somewhat irrationally, I wanted to feel the nearness of God in the hospital in tangible ways. I desired an Old Testament moment of my own. I wanted Jesus to appear in the middle of my mother's hospital room, with His clipboard, and explain what all of this was for. She had suffered a lot of pain and loss in her life already, and I could not fathom that this was how it would end.

From an early age I listened when she shared about the loss of her father and two brothers during the short span of three years. Her faith never waivered, even as sudden loss and terminal illness rocked her family.

I wondered if God saw all of the pain she had been through, and the anguish we were now experiencing. Sometimes considering our humanity in suffering is a better reflection of the reality of God. Becky McCoy says, "My father's cancer forced me to accept that death is a part of being human, which was an easy thing to accept. Grief was different. I thought that grief was a problem to be solved and not a human experience to process—I had to realize that emotions were part of being human, and they weren't flaws. I wanted to be Christlike, and I had assumed that meant flawless, but that's not being human—that's being God."

Expressing Grief in Front of Children

Jaime Jo Wright says expressing her grief in front of her children made her think twice. "My mom had asked us to come over after her diagnosis, and as soon as we got in the house I broke down. I cried like I've never cried before, and it freaked my husband out. When we got back home, I had a moment when I realized I couldn't do that again in front of my children. I didn't want them to see me grieving and think that I was without hope. I wanted them to see that though I grieved deeply, I would see my mother again, and so would they. I grieved, but with hope.

"Death would not steal her. This was the next stage in life, as my mother would put it. There was no sting in death, but there *is* pain. I promised myself I wouldn't break down in front of my family again, and I took it to the shower where I cried until the hot water ran out. The idea of her presence being absent was so stark in my mind, and I knew all that her absence would immensely change in our lives."

Grief is a personal experience that will express itself in each of us differently. For many, sharing your grieving experience with your children in an open way will allow space for your children to fully experience and process their own. Easier said than done. I found it difficult to cry in front of my children very often. When they did see me crying and asked what was wrong, I was honest. "I'm sad about Grandma. I'm having a hard time" was usually my reply. It also gave them the opportunity to practice their own empathy and express their love for me, which was a sweet balm during a very emotionally raw time. One of the most surprising outcomes of this experience was just how much I came to appreciate the warmth and love from my children. Many days I needed their little hugs more than they knew.

A Sweet Surprise and An Unlikely Friend

On the third day of her hospital stay, my mother's cousin, whose own mother had died a week before, walked into Mom's hospital room and handed her a small Bible. She said softly, "I found this in my mom's things as I was cleaning. Read the first page."

Mom opened the worn leather cover to see my late grandmother's handwriting on the yellowed page. It read: "For Carrie. Love, your mother."

My mother was devastated when my grandmother died nearly fifteen years prior. She often said she felt my grandmother's spirit with her during her most difficult moments. That Bible provided us all with the gentle hug from heaven we needed. If my mother's aunt had not passed only days earlier, that Bible never would have been found when we needed its comfort. It is still a mystery how the tiny Bible came to be in my great aunt's belongings. But God knew we would need it.

But God didn't stop there. Mom's first morning at home after her hospital stay began with an unexpected surprise. While my father brewed Mom her morning cup of coffee, he opened the curtains of the sliding glass door to the backyard. There, at the window, stood a peacock. Its head tilting side to side, it examined the living room inquisitively.

"Carrie, you have to see this!" Dad shouted.

Mom gingerly made her way to the window and gasped. The large bird pecked the window, as if to say *Hello*. Mom, a lifelong lover of all animals, sat next to the window and gazed back in awe.

Pecky the Peacock, as we came to know her because of her love for pecking the glass door, lived in my parents' backyard for several months before mysteriously flying away one day. During her time as part of our family, she loved dog kibble and napping by the sliding glass door next to Mom while she slept in her favorite recliner. It felt like a miraculous distraction—a sign that God was near and had a *great* sense of humor. He sent a large, random bird to let us know, and we were grateful.

These sorts of things often happen in the days following a crisis or even a death. Some may be tempted to label them as coincidence. For those of us who know the Lord closely, we know them to be the ways He shows us tangibly that He draws near to the brokenhearted and saves those crushed in spirit. It isn't always apparent what He has in mind as some of our worst days and moments swirl around us like a tornado, sweeping all normalcy and stability from our lives before we can take cover.

In those days, we hold to what we know: He has not left us. He knows the details and results of every scenario, every test, and every appointment. He is with us as a parent walks the path from our arms to His.

Telling Your Children

My boys loved their grandmother deeply, and she them. Her home was one filled with joy for the sake of joy. There were treats that only grandma had. She made friendship bracelets with my boys to give me as a surprise, and always had a wink to share with them—like they were in on secret hijinks too cool for me to know about.

Every time she left them with a big hug, she blew them a kiss for them to "put in their pocket." There were balloon races in the living room and coloring pictures at the kitchen table. At holiday dinners, my mom ate with her grandsons, and talked with them the whole time about what they loved. My mother excelled at being a grandparent. It was as though she had prepared her entire life for the role, and she thrived in it.

When her diagnosis shattered our lives, it was difficult for me to separate my feelings of grief and my sorrow about the pain I knew my children would endure at five and seven years old. When she died, I struggled to be the mother she encouraged me to be. She warned, "Don't let the grief swallow you. Love your babies. Spend time with your family. It all goes so fast."

My own grief and my boys' felt intertwined, a tangled ball of Christmas lights, too tightly wound to set right again. Inside it sat the memories they would never have with her, the ones they might forget, and the memories I would never witness being made. The heavy ball of tangled grief that sat unmovable on my chest would be a permanent part of my life now. I would have to make my peace with its weight.

My own grandmothers saw me grow up, and one lived long enough to hold both of my children. The memories I have are etched clearly in my mind—the way my mother's mother loved to underline her Bible, and how she smelled like rose-scented bath powder. The way my father's mother hugged me tightly, and always, *always* served mint chip ice cream after dinner.

I wanted so desperately for my sons to have the same. I wanted them to know her, not through my memories but through their own. A grandchild knows a grandparent differently than an adult child knows a parent. That kind of love is boundless and joyful. It revels in fun for the sake of fun.

Jaime Jo Wright's mother found a way to share her diagnosis with her grandchildren that brought joy, and even fun, into the equation. She says, "My kids were very close to their Nanny, and as soon as my mom knew we had told the kids about the cancer she asked us to bring them over. She met them at the door with a smile, like it was the biggest birthday party she was welcoming them to. She began talking to them about how excited she was. She said, 'This is what we all wait for when we begin loving Jesus. This is the most exciting thing, and you guys are going to help me get there.'

"I've had miscarriages, so she told them she would get there and see if they had any brothers or sisters. She told them she would start working on their heavenly houses and asked them what they wanted in their homes. My son told her he wanted a football field so they could play football together when he got there. 'Perfect,' she said. 'I'll be able to play then too.' She made everything into this great anticipation about her moving, and this was a large part of why I didn't want my grieving to distract from what she had just given them. Up until the day before she died, they were playing 'balloon wars' together. We wanted them to have and treasure as much time as they could with her. That's the last memory they have with her—playing balloon wars."

Mary Boswell's approach to sharing with her children involved including them in the day-to-day care for her mother. "When the cancer returned after her remission, we were very much upfront with them because we knew it was going to mean that all of us would be giving a lot of our time to help her. They would come with me to take care of her when they could, and my daughter would sometimes stay with me, as I had to move in with Mom at the end to take care of her. I remember both of their final moments saying goodbye to her. It was a sweet time."

Hope Anyway

I knew it was unlikely, but Mom was determined to be the first ever to beat her rare cancer. "I'm going to see the kids graduate high school," she would insist. We believed and hoped right along with her. I knew God could allow her to live if He chose.

And still, I knew my responsibility as a mother to prepare my children along the way for the more likely outcome. "Grandma is very sick. Right now, she looks the same, but over the next few months she might not," I said as matter-of-factly as I could. They asked the typical questions about doctors, and wondered aloud why medicine wouldn't cure her. "The doctors will give her medicine, and we hope it will make her feel better, but it probably won't take the cancer away completely," I said.

Then they asked the big question I knew was coming, the question I did not want to answer. "If she doesn't get better, will she die?" I remained steadfast in my matter of fact answering, though I was screaming internally about the unfairness of it all. "Yes, she will eventually die. But we are hoping for more time with Grandma, and that the medicine will make her feel better."

They handled the truth better than I expected, evidence that being honest is always the best route with children and difficult news. When they asked questions I didn't know the answer to, like why God would allow their grandma to be so sick, I admitted that too. "We don't always understand God's ways. The Bible says they are higher than ours. But we can know He has a good reason for it, even if we don't like it" was something I repeated a lot.

Being a Safe and Soft Place

I found there was a very fine line between informing them about what they needed to know and reminding them of the dreaded truth unnecessarily. Each night when we said our prayers as a family, I did not often include anything specific about her treatments or cancer. Those were prayers I kept between God and myself. We included her in our general prayers for family, just as we did other members, but I felt too much detail might place a heaviness on their shoulders that neither Mom nor God would want.

God knew my desperate pleas for her healing, and He also knew my deep desire for my children to be shielded from as much pain as possible. Resting in that truth was an act of faith.

I don't believe our children need us to be anything other than what we've always been—a safe and soft place. A place that is safe to ask questions without fear of upsetting you, and also a place to admit they are unsure how to be around their grandparent.

My older son, Bryce, six years old at the time, visited Mom in the hospital. Ed and I talked about it beforehand and knew the visit would bring joy to Mom, but we also weighed the impact on Bryce. She had an oxygen cannula, so we prepared him that Grandma might look a little different and would be in bed with some wires and tubes. He seemed a bit uneasy, but he wanted to see her.

Taking your child's preferences, temperament, and sensitivity into consideration will be key in making decisions like this for your children. My mother was adamant that we protect the boys' hearts at all costs throughout her illness.

Finding Joy

When Bryce arrived in her room, he timidly approached her bed and gave her a hug. The instant they embraced, it was as though we were back in her living room. "Want to get up here with me?" she asked. He nodded, and we lifted him into the bed beside her. "Want to take a ride? This bed is like a magic carpet!" she said while pushing buttons on the side and lifting and dropping the bed. Bryce giggled.

It was the joy we all needed to see. My heart needed to see my boy and my mom, enjoying one another even through the sorrow.

When she got home, we took both boys to see her. As expected, this was a more comfortable and anxiety-free visit.

My younger son, Bradley, nearly three, was too young to grasp the feeling in the room. Just as he always loved to do, he climbed into her recliner beside her and fell asleep with his head against her chest.

It was heartbreakingly beautiful for all of us to witness. Mom enjoyed a unique and deep bond with each of my boys, and it was important to me that we allowed them to deepen and grow that bond for as long as we could.

Every decision can feel a bit weighty at first, especially when our children are involved, but God asks us to trust Him with their hearts too. We still have the video of Bryce and Mom on their magic carpet ride. Though it is hard to watch now, I'm glad we have it.

Our children are adaptable, but don't be afraid to make choices about their exposure to this experience either. As parents, we are their protectors, so I encourage you to find the balance that works well for you and your family, even if others scoff at what you do or do not allow. You're the parent, and whether you feel like it or not, you do know your children best.

Is it Genetic?

It may not be your first thought when your parent has a terminal illness, but I'm certain concern about genetics will arrive at some point in the journey. I remember the moment I had the thought that made my stomach drop even farther to my feet—followed by a wave of guilt and shame. *What if I get this too? What if it's genetic?*

The fear swept over me in a warm wave when I imagined my children enduring the exact moment I was experiencing. *You're sitting in her hospital room, worried about yourself,* I scolded myself internally. The truth is, when you learn awful and unbelievable news *anything* feels possible. When anything feels possible, and therefore everything *could* happen, rationality goes out the window.

In my case, genetic testing of Mom's biopsy samples revealed that her cancer was not hereditary, which was a relief. That does not mean I won't develop something else down the line. After all, as they say, none of us makes it out of this life alive. The concern you might inherit your parent's condition is a valid one, and it shouldn't illicit guilt, though I know personally that it sometimes does.

If you are worried or your own scenario proved to be the opposite and your parent's condition *is* hereditary, I encourage you with this:

God alone is in control of every cell of your body, and He knows the future. No statistic or even genetic test can tell the future. Tests provide us only with a likelihood or unlikelihood, while Christ stands in the gap. He knows with certainty, and He will be with you regardless of the outcome.

We can rest in the truth of His faithfulness—of His with-us-ness. I don't say that lightly. There are times He feels far, but I have learned that feelings can and do lie. Our emotions do not dictate His proximity. Jesus is the same as He has always been—as close as our next breath. We can trust Him.

A Moment for Mindfulness

Telling our children about our parent's illness in age-appropriate ways is key, according to Licensed Clinical Social Worker Sherry Lewis. "When you're explaining the situation to your children, it may be wise to do so individually. Consider the emotional maturity of each child before broaching the topic and decide whether you need to speak to them separately. If you decide to tell them all at once, tailor your explanation to the youngest child's age. Explaining terminal illness to your children can be delicate, so saying something like, 'Grandpa has cancer, and generally if someone has this disease it is likely they will die of it,' is simple yet honest."

Lewis says using age-appropriate timelines is also important. "Small children don't have a good concept of time, but if you can use timeframes they are familiar with, it helps. Relating it to how many birthday parties a grandparent may have left, or even their own birthday celebrations, can help to frame it in an understandable way, if you're choosing to talk about life expectancy."

If children struggle to understand changes in the grandparent's behavior or ability to interact with them as usual, Lewis stresses the importance of making the explanation child-friendly. "You can say something like 'Grandma's body isn't able to do the same things it used to. It's like when a toy is running out of batteries, it doesn't work the same anymore.' Children typically understand this metaphor really well when it's put into those terms."

Consider:

- How would your children best comprehend your parent's diagnosis?
- What is the most gentle and truthful way to help them understand for their age?

A Daughter's Prayer

Lord, so much is uncertain. I feel heavy beneath the weight of my own grief and that of my children. The pain feels unbearable as I consider what is to come and what we have already endured. Please guide me as I aim to reflect You in every interaction on this new journey. I place my health, both future and present, into Your capable hands, Father. Help me to know how to best shelter and shepherd the hearts of my children, even as I know You shelter and shepherd them too. Thank you for the strength to stand on Your firm foundation. Amen.

THREE

THE MURKY MIDDLE:

THE EMOTIONAL ROLLERCOASTER OF CARE AND ARRANGEMENTS

> She is clothed with strength and dignity; she can laugh at the days to come.
>
> Proverbs 31:25

Willing my question to sound reasonable instead of desperate, I asked my mother's Stanford oncologist, "If this chemotherapy doesn't work, what is our next step?"

Mom's doctor was an esteemed physician who had a lovely rapport with her patients and their families. Mom instantly loved her.

"Then," she said, "there are three others we can try in different combinations. And if those aren't effective, there are always clinical trials. We won't give up."

Her answer quelled my endless need for reassurance that we could hope for more time—that maybe we could extend the countdown just a little longer. I spent countless hours researching online medical journals about possible treatments and survival statistics—enough to know that while the act of researching quenches your unending need to know what will happen *in the moment*, it's also vital to your mental health to know when to *stop*.

At a certain point, I realized that statistics were individuals, and my mother was also an individual. Behind every number is a human who had highs and lows along his or her journey—details we can't know from an article only delivering the awful truth in black and white. What mattered was what we could and would do for Mom, and part of that was maintaining hope.

God is bigger than cancer. God is bigger than any health condition in our human experience. Jesus healed leprosy, blindness, and reversed death itself, to name only a few. We could be realistic, but we could also keep real faith too.

If you find yourself researching hopeless statistics while your own hope begins to dim, I encourage you to step away from the Internet and do something that requires you to stand up, move your body in a way that feels good, and maybe even smile. God alone knows the future. It's not your responsibility to try to also. Our bodies are not meant to bear the mental and emotional weight of attempting to solve problems we aren't meant to solve. The consequences of taking God's work on as our own will show themselves through fatigue, anxiety, and insomnia. This is a time to let God be God.

Jesus Himself told us not to worry and asked, "Can any one of you by worrying add a single hour to your life?" (Matt. 6:27). In the same way, our worry will not add a single hour to the life of a parent. Psalm 139 in the NIV says, "Your eyes saw my unformed body; *all the days* ordained for me were written in your book before one of them came to be" (emphasis mine). Our parent's lives, as well as our own, have a certain number of days. Our worry will not affect what God has chosen.

A Word About Control

Researching treatments and learning the ins and outs of what may be ahead for your parent can bring a sense of action and helpfulness. It may not always be best to share with your parent unless they have given permission and the go-ahead to do so. Often, from my perspective, a new possible treatment seemed like the best news or option, but to my mother, it seemed like more poking and prodding. It was harder for her to get her hopes up. Some things I mentioned were out of the question because of travel or exorbitant cost.

I had to learn to accept that not everything I diligently researched and put forward would be considered a viable idea. This also applies to health supplements or foods I wanted her to try. When someone is sick with a terminal illness, often quality of life reigns over quantity, and in many cases, rightfully so. If you find yourself feeling discouraged because your parent seems "set in their ways" or hesitant to try what you suggest, remember that this is their life and their path.

As much as you might love for them to go sugar-free and use the new juicer you bought them for a cleanse you read about, it is ultimately their decision. One of the greatest gifts we can give our parents in their remaining time is the ability to call the shots and listen to their reasoning for decisions you may not always agree with.

Perhaps your parent has chosen to forego treatment all together, and you disagree with the choice. While this is painful and difficult to stomach as an adult child, I recommend that you first pray about your emotions that are likely running high. Give yourself a few days to sit with the news and consider what you would do in the same situation.

Maybe your choice would be different or the same. In either scenario, the most loving thing you can do is to share your thoughts with your parent. Then listen, truly listen, to what they say. This is another opportunity to love your parent through your actions, as difficult as it might be.

Supporting Them While They're Still Here

One afternoon, my mother told me about an event that night at a local church for cancer survivors a nurse had mentioned. She was reluctant to go, but I sensed she really wanted to. "If you want to go, Mom, then let's go!" I said. I convinced her it would be worth our time—a chance for a fun girls night out, just the two of us.

I picked her up as promised and together we drove to the church. When we entered, we saw women of all ages holding signs that displayed the amount of time they had survived cancer.

The mood was buoyant. Upbeat music blared in a nearby courtyard where women wearing pink and purple boas chatted and laughed.

Mom grinned from ear to ear. I saw a sense of pride wash over her as she took in the scene.

A woman put her arm around Mom at the door. "You have to be in the parade!"

Mom explained she just came for the event, but quickly learned if she had cancer, she was *in* the event. Inclusion. Just what she needed. She would not be on the outside looking in at survivors. She was going to *be* one.

I was grateful for these women I did not know—for this sisterhood that wrapped my mother in love, having not yet met her. They were Jesus in a pink feather boa.

I fought the lump in my throat the entire night. When the announcer declared the parade of survivors was to begin, people turned their attention to the corner of the room. My jaw dropped when I saw Mom was the first woman, radiant and holding a sign proudly that read: *Survivor, Two Weeks*. She walked with purpose and determination through the auditorium as I willed myself not to sob.

We cheered and applauded as woman after woman bearing the scars of a treacherous battle walked past. That night something shifted in my mother. She took ownership of the days ahead, no matter what they held. As her daughter, I vowed to never forget that evening. I wanted to always remember her this way—beaming with pride, with strength.

The most meaningful parts of this journey are often the unexpected and ordinary. Attending the event felt scary for me in many ways. To go was admitting that she had cancer and was fighting a battle like every other woman in that room. And that was exactly what made the event powerful for Mom. She saw others like her, fighting the battle and winning. She went from a woman diagnosed in a hospital to part of a community who knew what it was to hear the dreaded words and come out the other side into survivorship. It mattered not whether they had survived one minute or one year—they bore the title they had earned in tears and strength: Survivor.

All our parents are different—some may not want to attend an event with others. Some may need a little push to go, or someone to go with, like my mother. As a daughter who would choose a night at home over just about anything else, I encourage you to go with them to what is offered for their condition in your area if he or she is able. Put on your cute clothes, do your hair, and *go*.

In the end, supporting Mom as much as I could meant everything to *me*. I still hold regrets, as I suspect all of us will, of what more I could have done. But there are these moments, these memories that we hold in our minds forever, knowing that *when* we could, we did *what* we could.

Making Room for the Guest No One Wants

Perhaps you're trying to find the balance between supporting your parent and being present in the way you have always been with your family. Personally, I found that while I wanted to remain the same mother, wife, and daughter as before her diagnosis, it was impossible. This new member of the family—cancer—invaded our space, and it wasn't leaving.

I knew that the longer it stayed, the more it would invade our lives. It was a non-negotiable now, and denying the way it changed me, and our lives would be denying the growth and possible value God wanted to bring through it.

I had to make room for it, but I also kept strict boundaries for what it could and could not impact. Stealing my time with my kids by causing me to anxiously Google each of her new side effects for hours on end? Nope. A quick search to get a general idea of their possible harm would suffice.

Reminding me that because time was short, I should spend more time with Mom and Dad doing fun things whenever we could? Yes, that was an allowable impact of cancer. I would not allow it to steal more than it already had from our lives—and I would take whatever it had to offer me that added value to the journey.

Physical Scars

I still remember the day my mother went in to have a procedure to place her chemotherapy port. I had never seen one before, so I wasn't sure what to expect, even though the doctors made it seem as though it was a simple procedure. It was indeed a minor procedure, and Mom only experienced a little pain after the surgery.

What became the most apparent was we now had a visible reminder that she was sick. The port protruded from her chest, a small bump that clearly wasn't supposed to be there. I both resented it and was grateful for it, knowing it would be the vessel that brought my mother any possibility of more time with us. I hated that she now had to choose clothing that didn't irritate the area, even months after being placed.

We were now aware it might get infected. Each time she went for treatment I had the same thought: None of this process is easy. Her side effects each week of treatment made me wonder if it was truly worth what she was going through. But she was determined to give herself the best fighting chance for as much time as she could squeeze from her prognosis. But it was hard to watch her battle through nausea and exhaustion for days after her chemo infusions.

So much about a terminal illness can be surprising in the early days of treatment, even if symptoms were already present. Having physical signs of the disease make it all the more real. Surgical scars seem to shout, "There is no going back to the way it was. Here's a lasting mark to remind you of the fact." Weight loss and exhaustion remind us of the lack of rounded healthy smiles that now only grin back at us in picture frames.

Another Thing to Grieve

Along with the diagnosis itself, this too must be acknowledged as another little death of the way things were. It's alarming how much the physical body can change in such a short amount of time, and it's okay if you find yourself shocked and heartbroken by the difference. Along the way we discovered only more alarming changes that came our way— hair loss, the occasional draining of the fluid around her stomach, her skin jaundiced from liver failure, and the weight she spent much of her life wishing away, falling off her at a rapid pace. Each step of the way, the reminders continued to come, each more heartbreaking than the last.

Shifting Sands

There is no way around it—dying is ugly. Acknowledging the physical differences and grieving them when you need to is a necessary part of this journey. No one wants to witness suffering, and especially not the suffering of someone so dear. It's a gut-wrenching pain that leaves you feeling helpless.

This groundless time, when the sand beneath your feet is forever shifting with the tides of change, can leave you grasping for something solid. Sometimes, I found myself praying simple prayers, made up of very few words, because I had none to offer. *Jesus, You know*, was one I prayed often.

I believe in these wordless spaces of pain that Jesus rushes in to be with us even closer than before. Our broken hearts utter groans that only He can decipher, and in that moment of holy connection between our brokenness and His power, we find our strength renewed.

The pain is still painful, and the ache still threatens to overwhelm, but Jesus knows our limits. He knows what we can bear, and it is when it is too great, that He pulls up a seat next to us and shoulders what we cannot. He is present and He is faithful—our truest friend during our greatest need.

Gifts Along the Way

Though the physical marks of disease are hard to bear, God can also use them for encouragement in unexpected ways. My mother, who had been experiencing hair loss from chemotherapy and feeling self-conscious, decided to shave her head in an act of regaining some control over her body. She looked amazing with the lack of hair, to all our shock, and we told her so.

One afternoon, Mom called and excitedly told me about a holy experience she had just had at the *grocery store*. "Yes, they came to me right there in the yogurt section," she laughed and told me about the two older women who approached her. "They came up to me and asked if I had cancer, and I told them I did. Then they asked if they could pray for me, and I said they could," she explained with obvious delight in her voice. "One of the women began to pray a prayer for my complete healing, while the other one began singing the most beautiful song I've ever heard, though I couldn't tell you if it even had words. It sounded angelic. As they prayed and sang, I felt a warmth go from my head to my toes. It was incredible."

Then came perhaps the most meaningful part of the story. "They said they were on their way to a different grocery store, but felt God urge them to get off of the freeway right that moment, to go to this store—and then they saw me and knew I was who they were sent to pray for—isn't that crazy?"

The experience left my mother feeling seen and cared for by God in a way that lasted for the entirety of her illness. She would refer back to the story when she recalled all of the ways God had shown Himself to be faithful along the way, even if a complete healing never came on this side of heaven.

Perhaps this is how our most vulnerable moments become our strengths when placed into the hands of God. My mother's hair loss became confirmation to two souls who were willing to be His hands and feet, right there next to the strawberry Yoplait.

Though our parents bear the physical marks of illness, we bear the invisible. This is why I find it important that we be open about our unseen pain and sorrows as we are given the opportunity. We never know how God will use them to bless us or someone else. Strength can be found in shared experience—hopefully that is what you're finding while you read this book.

Our greatest weaknesses become vessels of strength, not because of our actions, but because of the God who loves us more than we can fathom. We are seen. We are known. We are held.

The Unsung Heroes

My mother and father lived almost two hours away from Stanford, and each week battled Bay Area freeways to get to treatment. I worried about my father, who loved my mother more than he hated Bay Area traffic and tirelessly drove her each week. Caregiver burnout is a real thing, and I worried it would all be too much. This is something many of us with terminal parents don't learn until we are in the middle of it—the toll it all takes on those that love them most.

For Quantrilla Ard, who was in college during the peak of her mother's illness, caregiving fell to her aunt. "I think it was really hard because her illness lasted so long. It took a huge toll on my family. I missed a lot of her later days. I had been away from home for four years on and off. I came home my freshman year and saw that she had an oxygen machine. My family didn't want to worry me while I was in school. I didn't ask many questions and they didn't offer information. Technically I was an adult at twenty-two, but I was not prepared to live without her. I didn't know that while I was away at school and preparing to graduate that I would only have a couple months with her when I came back home."

The Rollercoaster of Treatment and Disease Progression

If you know you know—there's a rollercoaster to this whole terminal diagnosis thing that no one tells you about until you're at the top and ready to plunge down the first dip. If treatment is available, and your parent is taking it, the entire process becomes a rhythm of anticipatory anxiety and relief or disappointment.

For my mother, it was three weeks of treatment, and then a one-week break. At each interval she would receive blood work or a CT scan, where the unspoken questions would linger in our minds: *Is treatment even working? Is it buying us any time?*

The morning of a scheduled scan, I would wake up with a familiar tightness in my stomach. A constant hum of anxiety followed me while I made my coffee, woke the boys, and made lunches and dinner. It was an unspeakable comfort that my brother and I had one another to lean on. We would text throughout the day, both of us held in the same breathless wait. And then it would come, a call or text from Mom: *It's working for now.* We focused on the first two words and not the last two.

Mary Boswell felt responsible in an unexpected way when she accompanied her mother to chemotherapy treatments. "I was a critical care nurse, so my heart has always been the heart of a caregiver. I noticed when we first began treatment, I felt like I needed to go into each treatment time not only taking care of her, but also the others receiving treatment there. It took a couple times for me to realize I didn't have to reach out and minister to everyone else in the room. The Lord was calling me to specifically care for my mom during that time."

Unexpected Hiccups in Treatment

Often treatment doesn't go as expected. My mother suffered an allergic reaction to chemotherapy as well as a clinical trial drug, and adjustments had to be made. The clinical trial drug was working marvelously for her cancer, but because of an adverse effect the doctors could not continue to offer it as a treatment option. It was frustrating and disheartening.

How I wished treatment were a straight line instead of a winding path I could never predict. It felt as though we could never quite keep her on a stable path for long enough, though the truth was that we wanted her on that path indefinitely. We knew at some point our options would run out, but we focused on the next step, as long as there was one.

Becky McCoy's father experienced something similar. "The doctors kept learning more information about Dad's condition, and things kept changing with his treatment plan. He tried chemotherapy but had a really bad reaction to the medication—so much so, they weren't sure he would survive it. My dad never gave up the fight, but we all knew he wasn't going to win this one. Still, we encouraged him to keep fighting, if that's what he needed."

In cases of dementia, the path to treatment can take longer as symptoms and diagnosis aren't always immediately clear. Sophie Hudson recalls, "By the time we had a diagnosis, it was like someone had given us a big piece to a puzzle, because there had been a couple years where Mama was just not herself, and I couldn't have said exactly why. She had always loved to talk on the phone and would call multiple times a week to catch up, but she stopped doing that with my siblings and me. She just increasingly wanted to be with Daddy. Mama's long-term memory was intact, and it was her short-term memory that was affected. She struggled with aphasia, which is a difficulty with speech. Watching her become more internally withdrawn was the hardest part. Once we knew what we were working with, the doctor was able to prescribe some medication as well as regulate some other medications so she felt better overall. It wasn't easy for my Daddy, who was her main caregiver, but he was remarkable in his patience and commitment to her through it all. When you're walking through it in real time, you just do the best you can."

Entering Hospice and Palliative Care

The thought of hospice and palliative care is sometimes hard to stomach, especially if your parent has been fighting their illness a long time. That type of care feels like the last stretch of a long race, but it can also feel like giving up.

In my experience, it was an option from the start because of Mom's diagnosis being imminently terminal, according to the first doctor. We had palliative care services at my parent's home, but when my mother began treatment and improved greatly, it was no longer needed. We waited until she needed hospice care to bring services back into the home about two months before she died.

It's important to know that often palliative care and even hospice services can be used for a time and then stopped if they are no longer needed. You can bring them back if needed.

Looking back, I can see that early on the services weren't necessary. My mother was still able to complete all of her daily living activities on her own, and the extra care had more of an impact on her mental health than anything else. Having a nurse in your home when it's too early is a daily reminder of the future that may not be healthy for your parent to constantly face. Having the least amount of change as possible will be the most encouraging thing when the situation hasn't become dire yet. Her independence from in-home healthcare gave Mom a sense of hope during treatment as it shrunk the tumors, that she was stronger than the doctors expected. The rest of us knew that already.

My experience with palliative care and hospice was a mostly positive one. We were pleased to learn the hospital bed and oxygen tank she would need would be brought to the house and set up free of charge to us, and that a medical team would be available around the clock by phone.

Becoming a patient of hospice meant that we no longer had to fight to obtain the pain medications we knew she required at that stage of illness, and all of our most difficult questions were given delicate and kind answers. By the time most patients reach hospice, they're worn out and weary of treatments and tests. Hospice, and even palliative care, is a time of rest and quiet. No more beeping machines and nurses shuffling in and out. Still, it's a struggle to accept at times that this is your reality.

On a weekly basis I sat in awe and numbness while I watched nurses treat my mother with gentle care. I wondered at their lack of hesitation in getting to know us as a family, and my mom as a patient. It felt like they must have otherworldly strength to do this repeatedly—to draw so close to a patient, only to say goodbye.

My mother's favorite nurse would refer to her as "Mom" to the rest of us, and openly shared her own experience of her father's journey to heaven. She answered my calls at midnight when I had to know whether a new symptom was cause for alarm. I know this was her job, but it never felt as such. Hospice and palliative care can be a wonderful experience, but if it isn't for your family, don't hesitate to change hospice care companies. We ourselves switched from one to another when the quality of care was lacking.

For Shay Mason, the road to receiving proper hospice and in home care was difficult. "After Dad got out of the hospital, he came home for about two weeks. My mom and I worked to push protein and fluids, because he was diagnosed with extreme malnutrition at the hospital that is typical for pancreatic cancer patients. He resisted eating and drinking, but we knew he couldn't have his next chemotherapy treatment without gaining weight. It was a battle each day and my mom, who is barely five feet tall, was struggling physically to care for him, because my father was a big man. We were told we would have coordinated in-home nursing care but the only people that came were an occupational and physical therapist and occasional help with bathing.

"He had already fallen a few times because of his blood pressure dropping because of dehydration, and she would take him back to the emergency room to be checked. After his last stay in the hospital, it was decided he qualified for in-patient hospice care because he was unable to swallow, which meant he could not take his medications at home. He wanted to be at home, but we knew this was the best choice for him. The ambulance came to take him to the hospice center, and with tears in his eyes he asked, 'Is this the end of the road?' We told him it was, but we were going to be with him. I can still feel that moment."

When Mary Boswell's mother's cancer returned for the second time, she knew it was different. "My mom was a miracle in that she lived three years after her diagnosis. Most of the time pancreatic cancer patients live only weeks to months. When we received the news that the cancer had returned, we knew immediately it was only a matter of time. Still, we tried the oral chemotherapy, and that lasted only a day. She did several weeks of radiation and then the time came for her to be placed in hospice. We didn't know how long she had, but we knew she had reached the end of her treatments. The day she met with the oncologist and made the decision was really therapeutic for her and my sister and I, though it sounds weird to say that."

This process of living in the middle of a parent's illness has a way of teaching an invaluable lesson—focusing on what is right in front of us instead of what lies farther ahead is vital to surviving the ups and downs with our minds intact. Isn't that what Jesus tried to convey when He said not to worry about tomorrow because each day has enough trouble of its own? Today is what we can do. This moment is all we can carry. It's enough. Our heads and hands and hearts cannot handle more. Tomorrow will have trouble, but let tomorrow be *tomorrow*.

While your parent is still here, you don't know it, but your mind and heart are on double-duty. You're handling the logistics of appointments and treatments while also wanting to keep them—and possibly your other parent—as comfortable and content as possible in an impossible time.

As the end draws closer, the strain it takes on you, your marriage, and your family is often overlooked, though you absolutely can sense its presence. I often felt as though I wanted to clone myself with one of my clones being able to sit at home and do absolutely nothing. It felt impossible to be at rest in my own skin, without the urge to be *doing* something. It is a lot of pressure to be the one, or one of a few, people who can take the reins and ask questions of hospice or treating doctors.

Some questions you might find helpful to ask are:

- What does your care protocol look like?
- At what point is palliative care or hospice recommended?
- What are the most likely side effects of these medications?
- What do we do if we need to change or add a medication?
- Are medications delivered, or will we need to use a pharmacy?
- Do we still go to the hospital for emergencies if my parent is on hospice care? Typically, you call hospice and stay home, but it is a good thing to clarify.
- How many nurses will be coming to the house on rotation?
- When can we call you, and is there a direct line to reach a nurse?
- What will his or her final weeks look like, and how will we know the end is drawing close?
- Does a doctor or nurse have to be present at the death, or can we keep that private if we like?

When No One Else Gets It

Some of the hardest moments of this experience are those when you feel no one else completely understands the place of anguish and stress your family is experiencing. From the diagnosis on, it can feel like the rest of the world offers a surface level comprehension at best. They understand that cancer will need chemotherapy or radiation. An Alzheimer's diagnosis will require in-home care, and a role reversal of parent and adult child. Heart failure or lung disease treatment includes palliative care.

What they won't understand is the rest of it—the weight you carry internally. The emotional rollercoaster of scan days and lab work. The nights spent worrying. The day trips to "get away from it all" that you spend pushing away the thoughts that intrude even during joyful moments. The trips to the grocery store to find food they'll be able to stomach. The smallest triggers that set off a new realization or ocean of tears.

These are the moments they may not grasp, through no fault of their own. Nurses and doctors are compassionate but keep themselves at a professional distance. They witness the awful experience you've just endured on a weekly if not daily basis. What is uniquely horrific to you, is another patient they did their best to diagnose and treat.

Family and friends try to find the words to somehow make it better, or at least not so dark. They bring casseroles and send cards. "I'm so sorry, Jen. Sending prayers to you all in this difficult time." I read these words repeatedly, and every time they made me cry. Not that I did not appreciate the sentiment—truly, I did. They brought forward the reality that it was all actually happening. *I* used to be the one who sent those types of messages to *others*. And now it was *me* on the receiving end. It was humbling. The helper now needed help.

On the other side of things, I remembered all the times I offered thoughts and prayers to others while they endured this deep pain I had no concept of at the time. To say my eyes were now opened was an understatement. The simple truth is that no words will ease the sort of pain a poor diagnosis and prognosis elicits in a family. I now know it's better to state that simple fact: There are *no* words.

I found the most comfort in those who knew what we were going through because they had experienced it themselves. *Those* were the words that made me feel less isolated. They had called compassionless insurance companies and asked bored medical receptionists to transfer records. They bought laxatives and gas medication to help digestive issues from heavy pain medications. They knew what it was like to see women and men the same age as their loved one and grow resentful that they likely had a long life ahead of them.

My brother and I laughed at our internal annoyance directed toward elderly people taking walks or gardening. Who exactly did they think they *were*, still living past their sixties? They knew the unspoken heaviness that now sat upon my shoulders, even when my mouth smiled or laughed. Always present, always there, like the most obnoxious and depressing houseguest that never takes a cue to leave.

If you're feeling isolated, that's a valid feeling. This is a lonely road, that in truth, we each travel in our own way, while often seeing the same scenery. The only one who truly knows our unique experience is Jesus because He's been with us every second. He's the one friend we need not explain the way our brain travels to the worst-case scenario like it's the only neurological path it knows. He knows it all—from the nurse who showed such compassion you were certain she was Him in different form to the evenings you spend sobbing in the shower so your family doesn't worry about you more than they need to. It's okay if you can't find the words to explain your complicated and aching heart—He already knows.

A Moment for Mindfulness

One of the most difficult feelings when a parent is sick, is the pressure to do our very best when it comes to ensuring they receive the best care and treatment, all while continuing to handle our own needs and those of our family. Licensed Marriage and Family Therapist and Author, Nicole Zasowski, advises that we create a visible reminder for ourselves to focus on what is actually in our control. "Be very aware of what you can and cannot control—pain has a way of making it abundantly clear what we cannot. Life is not a formula, and no matter how much we work or pray about something, it won't change the reality of that fact.

"Anxiety is a sign that our brain is trying to control something that is impossible to control. I recommend this exercise in my practice: On a piece of paper, draw two large circles. Label one 'Things I have been empowered to do' and the other, 'Things I would love to control and I can't.' When you're finished, you'll see that the items in the last circle, that you wish you could control but can't, are things you can only pray about. Our energy is best spent on the things we can control, the items in our circle of influence when we want to start controlling the ups and downs of the situation."

Consider:

- How is your mind trying to control the uncontrollable?
- Where can you place the circle exercise in your home to remind you of what you can control and what you need to pray about instead?

A Daughter's Prayer

Lord, the ups and downs of this road are hard to bear. My anxious mind constantly fears the worst and tries to prepare me for it too. Father, prepare my heart through your grace and compassion. Give me deep relaxing breaths when it feels impossible to breathe. Only You understand this wilderness. And yet, I feel so alone in this grief and pain. Come into this lonely space, and let me feel your presence, Lord. I know You love me and my family deeply. Please reveal yourself to us, in ways we will only recognize as You. Amen.

FOUR
THE LASTS AND FIRSTS: HOLDING HOPE IN UNCERTAINTY AND SORROW

> Your eyes saw my unformed body, all the days ordained for me were written in Your book before one of them came to be.
> Psalm 139:16

Handing Mom a yellow gift bag, I strongly suggested, "We need you to open this gift immediately—like right now."

She sat in a chair under an umbrella on the beach in Carmel, a favorite place to visit for as long as I can remember. It was her sixty-third birthday, and she had been diagnosed the month before. She was getting her chemotherapy port in two days. I marveled at how she agreed to a beach trip when the beginning of an unknown and terrifying journey began in less than forty-eight hours. I wondered silently if I would be so strong.

We all gathered around her, Dad, Zach and his wife Berenice, Ed, and our boys. All of us knew what that gift bag held except for Mom and Dad. We felt an excitement we could hardly conceal—my own hands and voice shook when I handed her the gift.

She peered inside and reached in. "Oh!" she managed to say before pulling out the tiny, squirming ball of fur and dissolving into tears.

We watched in tearful joy while my parents met their new puppy with an elation none of us had witnessed in a very long time. Zach and

I had decided weeks before that our parents needed something—anything—to take their minds off of all things illness, and a six-week old Shih-Tzu puppy fit the bill quite nicely.

We went out for dinner that night and watched my mom dance while the staff sang "Happy Birthday" to her. She threw back her head and laughed. Diners and the staff erupted in applause. They placed a surprise dessert in front of her—a peacock made of pineapple and other fruits.

Only God would send a peacock to her window and give her a peacock shaped dessert for her birthday. It felt like the kind of day that none of us anticipated we would ever have again when we heard the dreaded word "cancer." It was on that trip we learned in a real way that joy still exists in the midst of pain.

All of us were terrified of what the next months held for my mother. But for that day, we surrendered to the joy of the present. We had cried in hospital rooms and surrendered to grief in the weeks prior. And we did the same for joy that day.

Contrary to popular belief, a puppy won't fix everything. And now I'm certainly not an advocate of springing new pets on unsuspecting owners. We knew my parents wanted a dog and would be up for the task of pet ownership. I suspected the dog would become a true friend to my father after my mom was gone, and I was correct.

A few days after the trip, I convinced Ed that I needed the last remaining puppy from the litter in the worst way, and then we, too, became the owners of a Shih Tzu puppy, her brother whom we named Bailey. Those dogs have given us limitless joy and laughter over the years—a true gift from God. They were born two days before Mom was diagnosed, and I like to think they were meant for us all along.

In times of grief and shock, joy may be the last thing on your mind. I encourage you, though, to go find it. Allow yourself to be silly with your family, and to laugh. Life isn't meant to be taken so seriously, at least not all the time.

There is always something to be done to bring light into even the darkest of spaces. Consider what your parent finds hilarious or heartwarming. A change of scenery can do wonders as well, for everyone. Is there a place of beauty nearby you could travel with your parent to, and remind each of you that good times are still possible? Every circumstance is different, and only you know yours. Regardless of the time your parent has left, it *is* possible to think of it as living with a disease, instead of dying from it. Make the most of the good moments any way you can, while you can.

Trusting God to Provide the Hope

One of the most unexpected and faith-building experiences for me personally was the phenomenon of God providing me with comfort and hope in the most personalized and specific ways. During Mom's treatment I was freelance writing for *Reader's Digest,* and my editors, unaware of my mother's diagnosis, began assigning me article after article about cancer or cutting-edge treatments. I interviewed doctors and medical researchers on the cutting edge of cancer treatment, and spoke with cancer patients with miraculous recovery stories. When I shared with them my mother's diagnosis, it provided a common experience for the patients and I to bond over, and it made them more comfortable sharing their story with me—they knew I understood in a different way.

When I mentioned it to the experts, they generously offered to do anything they could for my family should I ever need a connection or help accessing treatment for Mom. The encouragement I gained after each of these conversations was then passed on to my parents, who I would excitedly share the latest therapy discoveries and breakthroughs with. It was a fresh dose of hope, enough to get us through until we needed more. Only God would know what I needed at that time, and He was so gracious to connect me with these generous souls. I learned in a profound way that most people, at their core, are deeply good and kind—they are reflections of God Himself.

If you're feeling fresh out of hope, or you have it now but worry it will be gone eventually, I want to assure you that just like manna in the wilderness, God continues to provide exactly what you need at exactly the right time. We can trust Him to do the unimaginable—what we aren't even aware that we need. He is always working on our behalf, preparing the connections and comfort you'll require along the way. You can rest knowing He's got it, and you, covered.

The Lasts

When your parent has been given a specific timeline for the remainder of their life, it can feel as though you're living the worst kind of countdown. Everything becomes the maybe-last. You might think, This is maybe the last Christmas, maybe the last birthday.

Holding onto hope when death feels relatively imminent is difficult, but it is worth the fight to remain in the present. There is an awareness that comes with a terminal diagnosis that isn't exactly pleasant but feels necessary. Today is all we have—every single one of us. That truth becomes both a comfort and a motivator, to be the best and kindest version of yourself to all you meet.

Every holiday and typical day in between is another opportunity to love your parent the way you want, regardless of what your past relationship looks like. It takes a conscious sort of training of the mind to refuse to give in to the thoughts that shout about the lasts.

I would be lying if I said that each of those three Christmas mornings I didn't think about it being the last we would celebrate as a complete family with my mom present. Every time she hugged my boys, or gave me a gentle squeeze at the door, I wondered how many more we would get this side of heaven. And each time my mind would rush to a future without her, I forced myself to come back to the present, because that's all any of us really had. I reminded myself over the nearly three years she survived after her diagnosis that we were certain the Mother's Day weekend she was diagnosed on was our last, and we still were together for holidays despite the odds.

On our final Christmas together, Mom gifted me a soft pink cardigan. We laughed that it was both fitting for my cozy at-home style, and also could have been given to an eighty-year-old. I tucked it in my closet, knowing that one day it would be needed. She died three months later. The next winter, I finally pulled the sweater out to wear. It felt like a warm hug she knew I would need without her here. *Moms always know,*

I thought as I wrapped it around my shoulders and tears sprung to my eyes. She was gone, but she was still wrapping me in her love.

For some of us, the treatment itself brings up feelings of fear and "what if" questions of time remaining. Mary Boswell recalls, "We had a family reunion that was right before her Whipple procedure, and it was a huge deal. We weren't sure that she would make it through surgery. We wondered how long she would survive after the surgery too, because there was no guarantee of post-surgery recovery either. We went to the family reunion with a sort of 'carpe diem' mentality. We wanted to seize the day and enjoy whatever moments we had because the time with her felt so God-given. The truth is, not everyone gets to know they're in the final days with someone they love. I processed a lot of emotion in the time leading up to that family reunion. Once we got past that, every Christmas we thought, *Is this it?*"

The knowing of being in the final days or moments with your parent feels like a holy understanding— a bridge you can see ahead that you and your parent will cross in different ways, but you will cross it all the same. Sophie Hudson says, "I was really mindful when she was in the ICU that this was probably my last chance to just love my mama well. I wanted to look back on it and have no regrets. I suppose that's a really good philosophy for humans in general, when it comes down to it."

My mother's last outing was to visit the cemetery plot we had chosen for her. She insisted my father, brother, and I make all the funeral and burial arrangements in the weeks preceding her death, knowing our minds and hers would be more at peace once it was finished. Through it all, her 'nothing is off limits' sense of humor never wavered. When I mentioned that some people chose cremation and kept some of their loved ones' ashes in a vial to wear as a necklace, she laughed. "Maybe they could just cremate one of my toes, and you could have it in a vial, a sort of lucky rabbit's foot?"

We chose a lovely oak tree-shaded spot at the local cemetery. The meeting with the funeral home was as pleasant as it could be, though the entire time I could not shake the unsettled feeling of how big of a business dying has become. When we helped mom out of the car and into the wheelchair to show her the spot, I saw her face become peaceful. She loved where we had chosen, and again, I marveled at her strength and resolve. Smiling, she said, "You can come and have a picnic with me out here sometime."

When we know our time together is shortened, we choose our words carefully. The things that would have upset us before the diagnosis may still ruffle our feathers, but our response is different. We have the big picture perspective now, a sort of holy gift we wish we had all the time. Jesus knew He was going to die and explained it multiple times to His disciples. Their response was confusion and fear, and even a vow to die with Him.

The known proximity of death changes our perspective. Our love for our parent becomes more evident than ever, as well as our longing for an eternity spent together. What Jesus said to His disciples, He still says to us, today: "Now is your time of grief, but I will see you again and you will rejoice, and no one will take away your joy" (John 16:22). A time is coming when we will see Him and our loved ones again, the pain of loss only a memory we faintly recall, if at all.

The Firsts

I often think about the first year without Mom on earth and feel bittersweet. I felt groundless and a little lost in so many ways, searching for a way to be in the world without my mother here as an anchor. Yet, there was still a closeness I felt to her then, as if she were only away for a short time. Her voice still fresh in my memory, she had only just left.

With each holiday or birthday that came, I spent the days leading up to it feeling a low hum of anxiety and dread. *This is going to be so hard without Mom,* I'd think and brace myself for the grief I knew was coming, or in some cases, had already arrived. We gathered for Easter as a family the week after Mom's funeral. We plastered our faces with smiles and tried not to think about the way our event was missing her exuberant laugh, and the scent of her favorite perfume wafting through the air as my boys hunted for eggs.

This is how it is now. This is how it will always be. The thought of this gaping void now being present at every holiday and family gathering made me feel like I were internally gasping for air. Still, I knew I had to keep going through the motions, hoping that one day it wouldn't feel so difficult.

I remembered her words to me, only half-joking, "You have twenty-four hours to grieve, after that, get on with living your life. Life is too short, Jen."

My mother knew loss and grief more than most, and now, looking back, I can see how she was teaching me to cope. And every birthday and holiday since, that's what I've done. We talk about her and laugh about what she would have said or done. I purchased Christmas ornaments that we place on the tree each year in her memory—hummingbirds, her favorite bird that mysteriously always find their way into our paths at important or poignant moments. I make her famous mashed potatoes and gravy each Thanksgiving and Christmas, though I haven't attempted her incredible fried chicken yet. The first Thanksgiving I tried to make her gravy. It took three batches to get it right. Still, each time, I could feel her presence cheering me on, knowing that my heart was to honor her still.

Each of these holidays, especially in the second year after her death, came with an inevitable moment of tears and allowing the grief to spill over. I tried, and still try, to focus on the moments in between the times when her loss feels like a physical ache. As time goes on, the stretches between grow longer.

Grieving During a Pandemic

My mother died in the early stages of the COVID-19 pandemic, and it felt very much as though my world was changing along with the rest of the population on earth. COVID-19 changed how we celebrated holidays. Gone were the gatherings with extended family that marked each year. Still reeling from loss, we now celebrated with our immediate family. The smaller celebrations were comforting in some ways. We weren't the only family with holidays that looked different. Nothing looked the same for anyone, and I wouldn't be faced with grieving her absence at big family Christmas celebrations or other events. It was one small reprieve in a time of utter chaos.

If you dread gatherings with family that your parent used to attend, I would encourage you to build in some safeguards ahead of time. Are there ways you can prepare yourself for the moments when the loss will loom larger? It won't take away the grief while you're there, but I have found comfort in shedding some tears ahead of time as a sort of release. It allows me to feel more present and peaceful when the day comes. Honoring your parent by bringing a special food or a beloved game they enjoyed can also feel like you're still including them in the family event.

I knew it would feel bittersweet, and I was correct. My mother was a sort of anchor for me at family gatherings. If there was no one free to talk to, she was there. If she was having a fun conversation with an aunt, I was always welcomed to join. If there was no other seating, I could be sure she would make room.

She was the first to hug my boys when we arrived, and always made them feel like the most important party attendees at any event. Her absence felt jolting. While I stood in my aunt's backyard and gazed at all the familiar faces, I felt the tears sting the back of my eyes. *She should be here,* I thought. *I'm alone.* The rest of my family was nearby, but it's a different kind of lonely to be surrounded but without your beloved parent. It surprised me that even years after her passing I was still discovering new ways of missing her.

Becky McCoy found that doing something different was helpful the year following her father's death. "The anticipation was the worst, so that first Christmas we had all my husband's family over because we had always done Christmas at my parent's home. I'm the oldest and my sister was still in college, and so we always stayed at their house for the holiday. That year, my husband's parents and sister and her family came to my parents' house for Christmas, so it wasn't just us that year. I think we were all afraid of feeling a gaping hole. We still felt his absence, but having extra people there and doing something a little different was really good for us."

Still, every holiday, no matter how different it now looks, and especially my birthday, I will have a moment of grief. The days leading up to the actual day are still a bit tense in my heart, waiting for the full wave of grief to hit. Sometimes that looks like memories that leave me teary-eyed and yearning for one more conversation with her. Sometimes it looks like a good cry in the shower. I've learned on these days more than anything, that no matter how it arrives, the grief subsides, and more often than not, the lead up to the day is much worse than the day itself.

This held true for the first anniversary of her death as well. My body remembered exactly where it had been the previous year, and my mind replayed scenes of those days leading up to her death like a movie.

I felt exhausted, almost exactly as I had been the year prior as my brother and I got very little sleep and sat vigil with her in the early morning hours. Though it was unsettling, it also felt like it was a necessary process for my body to take itself through. There was also a sweetness in remembering my last moments with my mom, as well as recognizing I had indeed survived an entire year without her physical presence in my life. The tears I shed in the days before helped to clear the way for a celebration or remembrance unhindered by overwhelming pain. I felt the loss, but I was not overcome by it.

Becky Keife also felt as though her body and mind responded to memories without her knowing. "It was like my body had a calendar of grief that would often present itself before I was logically aware of the reason I was stressed or irritable or depressed. It happens on my dad's birthday and Christmas, which was the last time we saw him alive. It happens again on the anniversary of his death, Father's Day, and then my birthday too. I begin feeling off about a week before and wonder why I feel so down, like I have a blanket of sadness covering me. It took some time for me to realize that the unnamed sadness or just feeling in a funk is actually grief. Realizing my body has its own grief clock is somehow comforting—an assurance that my loss matters, and each milestone is significant ... even as life just keeps going on."

...

Mary Boswell experienced something similar. "The first year after she (Mom) died, because I'm a critical care nurse and I walked through her illness with her, I thought that I was also walking through the grief process of her death at the same time. I didn't expect that first year after to be so hard. Her birthday was soon after she died, and the anticipation leading up to the day was so much more difficult than the actual day. The lead up would absolutely undo me—the days before that first birthday, Thanksgiving, Christmas, Mother's Day, Easter, were so much harder for me to get through."

For some, a change in perspective is enough to quell overwhelming grief. Jaime Jo Wright says, "I can either choose to look at the moments without my mom and focus on what I no longer have, or I can choose to focus on what I'm going to have with her in eternity. Every first without her, my goal has been to look at what I have coming up. Every year on my birthday, I think, I'm one year closer to spending it with her again."

No matter what you think the lasts and firsts with and without your parent may look like, I can assure you of this: You will get through them. There is grace enough for every step, even when they are new and unknown. Perhaps that is the most disconcerting part of this journey—the unknown.

Today, perhaps this very moment, someone somewhere is receiving life-changing news they never expected—a loved one taken in an instant with no warning, or a terminal diagnosis that seemingly came out of the blue. Nothing in this life on earth is certain except that it does not last. And so, we cling to the One who lasts forever, and therefore allows us to do the same in the next life. It is a worthy adventure to take, this temporary life with God by our side and in our very breath. He is with us.

A Moment for Mindfulness

According to Licensed Clinical Social Worker Sherry Lewis, handling the anxiety that the last times with someone may bring comes down to acknowledgement. "If you can acknowledge the truth—that this may be your last holiday or occasion with someone—both internally and externally—it takes the power out of the anxiety. Saying out loud, to someone you trust, 'This may be the last time we do this' helps you to process this fact and allows you to be proactive about the memories you want to make during this time. I caution against the tendency to have unrealistic expectations about making memories or changing traditions. Don't try to do something you've never done before. Keep it simple and in line with the traditional ways you've celebrated in the past. That's what you will remember—what you always did at that celebration or holiday. You can take more photos than you typically would but work to stay present in the moment too."

Grief that can show up during a last celebration should also be acknowledged, Lewis says. "If you need to, take a moment alone to be in the grief and then come back to the present. You can remind yourself, 'This is happening (a parent dying), but it's not happening right now.' It may be helpful to set a timer, allowing yourself to cry or journal for a brief period of time before returning to the celebration with the others. Imagine yourself shelving the grief or putting it in a box you can take down later. You're not ignoring it, you're waiting until a better time to give it more attention. I use the analogy of blowing up a balloon. If you continue blowing air into a balloon and never release any, the balloon eventually explodes. If you release the air, you can continue to add more in—the goal is to avoid stuffing it all and to release it at appropriate times."

If you're concerned about impromptu grief during times that aren't ideal, and you like to be alone during those moments, Lewis recommends having a plan. "If you're triggered in grief, it can be helpful to have a few coping skills to help you get it out and process it well. It can also be helpful to take note of what your grief triggers may include, such as a song, smell, or even taste that can trigger memories requiring more emotional and mental energy to cope with. You can have a code word with your partner that lets them know you'll be taking a few moments to yourself, or you can go for a walk to release some of that energy in your body. Different things will work for different people and the way they process grief personally."

Consider:

- What would help you feel as though you celebrated occasions well with your parent at the end of their life?
- What are some activities that work well for you to process your feelings, even if you're short on time?
- What grief triggers can you prepare yourself for ahead of time?

A Daughter's Prayer

Father, we measure time differently than You do. Still, I know that the time spent with and without my parent is precious to You. You see how I struggle in the celebrations I know are my last with my parent. How I desperately try to squeeze the time I thought we had left into the limits my parent now faces. You see me grieve in the quiet moments now that they are gone and how I long for things to be the same once again. Oh, how I yearn for the time before illness had a place in my parent's life, Father. I thank you for the promise that all will be restored again, even if it feels far away in this moment. Help me to feel Your love in my weakest moments. Guide me in how You would have me spend my time now, Father. Amen.

FIVE

ANTICIPATING THE IMPOSSIBLE: LOVING YOURSELF BY PREPARING FOR FUTURE GRIEF

> I would always look for clues to her in books and poems, I realized. I would always search for echoes of the lost person, the scraps of words and breath, the silken ties that say, Look: she existed.
>
> Meghan O'Rourke, "Story's End"

I sobbed into the phone, feeling both relief and guilt for unloading my own pain onto my mother's already heavy shoulders, "I'm going to miss you so much." I needed to say the words, to get them out, and as a mother myself I knew the heartbreak they must have caused her.

After she gave me comfort that only a mother can provide, we ended the call. I found the unyielding urge to write down every word of our conversations odd at first, and then decided to give in. I found an unused journal I had been saving for a special occasion and wrote down all that had been said word for word. *Someday I will need to see and remember that we said these things. Someday I will need to reread the words she just said, and they will comfort me when she can't.* I wrote until every word was recorded and breathed a deep sigh of relief. It would be there when I needed it. She, in some form, would be there, when I needed her.

I wanted to know about her family that had long since passed, I wanted to hear how she coped with her own father's death at only seventeen. I knew it wasn't completely possible, but deep down I hoped if I knew as much as I could and stored it in my mind and heart, that I wouldn't feel like I lost her entirely when she died. Every time I imagined our lives without her, it felt like I stood on the edge of a cliff, knowing the ground would eventually give way beneath me. I was terrified of where I would land, where all of us would land.

Imagining life without your parent reveals various reactions. While I felt the urge to record every moment I could in photos and writing, I also knew I didn't want to be that weird person suddenly following her every move when we were together. I wanted to prepare myself somehow for the loss of her while she was still with us, hoping that it would soften the sharp edges I knew my heart would break into. I also knew I would need to find a way to preserve memories of her for my boys.

A friend recommended I buy recordable storybooks to have her voice saved long-term for them. I bought the books, and she recorded her voice, inviting my older son to sit in the rocking chair with her as she read. It was a gut-wrenching moment, knowing that my son only thought she was reading him a story, and me knowing it was the last time she most likely would. Looking back, it was a gift we did this early, before chemotherapy treatments and advancing cancer made her voice hoarse.

On my first Mother's Day, five years before she was diagnosed, she gifted me with a memory book of her own childhood and adult memories, both prior to and after my birth. The gift of this book at the time was a beautiful thought. I had no way of knowing how much it would mean to me after she was gone. I now encourage anyone I can to make a memory book of some type for their children, even if they're not yet grown.

While your desire to prepare yourself in some way for your parent's passing may differ, here are some ideas that may give you a sense of doing something now to love your future self:

- Ask your parent to write you a letter, if possible, including whatever they want you to remember after they are gone.

- Record their voice or save voicemails. Even if you can't bring yourself to listen to them for a long while, you will be glad you have them.
- Take screenshots of special texts to one another, especially if they contain a conversation you will want to remember having.
- Take videos of everyday moments at home. You will want to remember their little quirks and habits that can fade with time.
- Schedule a family photo shoot or have someone close to your family come and take family photos, even if no one is feeling like it or you're not in your dress clothes. Make sure to get a photo of each person and your parent alone.
- Ask your parent to make you a playlist or a written list of their favorite songs.
- Purchase a memory book with fun questions. If they are too weak to write the answers, offer to do it for them. It makes for lots of laughter and fun conversation.
- Purchase books about grieving a death in advance, it may serve as a comfort to you to know they are there for you when you need them.
- Have your parent choose a special stuffed toy for each of your children that is meaningful and have them "pre-load" it with hugs and kisses. This is especially vital for younger children who may need something tangible to associate with their beloved grandparent when they are no longer able to hug or receive affection from them. You can also make toys from your parent's clothing after they pass for your children, but I have found that for my children it was actually less traumatic to have toys my mother owned instead of using her clothing.
- Have a discussion with your parent about items they may wish to have distributed amongst family members after their passing. This helps eliminate questions or even future disagreements about who gets what.
- Begin recording the memories your children are making with their grandparent in writing or through photos and video.

For some, it's enough to stay in the moment—to experience it all as it happens. This was the case for Jaime Jo Wright. "My mom would forget her camera and then say, 'I'm going to take pictures with my heart.' And that's what I tried to do, is just take a lot of pictures with my heart."

Life Events in the Middle of It All

Life goes on, as they say, even when the end nears for your parent. There are still jobs to go to, work to be done, and dreams to be accomplished, right in the middle of the unthinkable. After my mom's diagnosis, I continued to write and pursue the publication of my first book. Working to accomplish a dream during this painful time helped me remember that dreaming even a dream that felt impossible was still worthy of my time. It kept me focused on something other than illness, treatments, and prognosis. When the book was published and I got to experience the moment my mother—who was the biggest encourager of my writing—held my first book in her hands, it felt like an extravagant gift from God.

When my brother got married, it gave all of us a break from what felt like an unending teeter totter of cancer highs and lows. This was an event we could focus on with joy and excitement. My mother spent her time creating wedding favors and shopping for the perfect dress to wear. She found a wig that looked beautiful on her and made her feel confident. When she and my brother danced during the Mother-Son dance, there wasn't a dry eye to be found. And again, it felt like an extravagant gift to see my mother and brother have this moment.

A terminal diagnosis has a way of convincing us that joy is gone for the foreseeable future. We learn along the way that in actuality, it teaches us that life is lived in moments, not chunks of time. Every moment is an opportunity to step in faith where there is no sight. We can't know if our parent will be there to celebrate the big moments we yearn for, but that doesn't mean we should shelve them and not try.

What dreams are you working toward, even during the worry or sorrow of illness? If there aren't any, I encourage you to find something that brings you joy or motivates you to achieve a goal of some sort. It is in these seemingly small ways that we give our brains and hearts a bit of rest. Something else to focus your attention on that is just for you goes a long way to help you feel more balanced and light in a heavy time.

Anticipatory Grief

Anticipatory grief is a real thing, and as much as I would love to tell you it lessens the grief in the long run, I cannot. How I wish that were true. If it were, I would not have had a single tear to cry since Mom left us.

What I can tell you is that it makes this process more bearable and allows you to be a healthier version of yourself for your family as you endure the difficult times. For me, grief was always triggered when I allowed myself to wonder who I would call when I needed help, if my husband was unable to help me for whatever reason. I've had anxiety all my life, and as a little girl I depended on my mother to quell it. As an adult I was externally independent, but internally I still felt as though I desperately needed my mom. *Who will I call when I'm worried about one of the boys and I need her opinion? When I'm sick? Who will tell me to take a nap, to take it easy on myself?*

The thoughts never failed to bring tears to my eyes and an ache to my chest. I know the answers to these questions now. My mother's voice is so much a part of me that I can hear what she would say in each scenario I face. In this way, she is still very much with me. I did not know it then. I couldn't have.

Our parents never truly leave us. Even so, it was necessary that I allowed myself to explore the deepest questions my heart wanted answers for but couldn't find. Sometimes, it was helpful for me to talk to Mom about them while she was still here, to hear her reassure me that she would still be with me in some way.

As much as you are tempted to keep a strong front for your family, I encourage you to find a good place to fall apart. For me it was the car or the shower, or while washing dishes when I had a moment to myself. I never wanted my boys to see me cry, and in hindsight it would have been fine and healthy if they had.

Anticipatory grief made itself known in other ways than tears, of course. I would have less patience during the day—especially if it was the week of an important scan or the beginning of a new treatment. The weight on my shoulders to make everything okay for everyone felt heavy. And no one asked me to do that. It's impossible to make things okay when things are things are in fact, *extremely* not okay. The best we can really do is try not to make them worse, and if you aren't letting your grief out along the way, there's a good chance you will.

What I never realized at the time, is that after a terminal diagnosis, a family goes through many little deaths before anyone actually dies. There was the death of our sense of normalcy—the shock that our close-knit family was going to be missing its center soon. There was the death of freedom for my parents. Both retired, their dreams of traveling frequently came to a halt when weekly treatments and recovery from treatments ate up their time and energy. There were the many memories I expected to make with my complete family by my side—our boys growing older, marrying, a lifetime of holidays and laughter and beach trips—now gone. My mother's energy now drained from treatment, there would be no more playtimes with Grandma, or balloon races across the living room. All were gone, stolen by a disease we never saw coming.

Much of life during this time felt surreal. Was this really happening to our family? My mind took a bit to fully wrap around our new reality, and even then I don't believe I completely grasped it. It was too much to take in.

The importance of grieving these little deaths cannot be overestimated. You may not know consciously the reason for your tears or sorrow. Perhaps you are more of a logical person than an emotional one, and you understand that parents don't live forever, so you wonder, *Where are these tears coming from?* While your brain may know the facts and reality, your heart and soul know that these small things are worth your tears and time to process. Your grief is tied to your healing, and your body knows what is required. You can trust it.

You may find that the weirdest of things trigger you—a random memory or inside joke you'll miss sharing with your mom or dad. Let the tears flow whenever and however you can. Jesus wept, and so must we. It's an expression of both sorrow and great love, a gift to allow a healthier grieving process.

For Shay Mason, the anticipatory grief became overwhelming in a hospital parking garage. "It was after my father realized he had stage four cancer for the first time. He said, 'So that's why I feel like this.' I went out to the parking garage, and it was the first time in all this that I just lost it. I knew we were nearing the end, and I was just sobbing in the parking lot all by myself. I cried myself to sleep that night. I did that the first few nights. I would get home from seeing him and just be a wreck. Our church was amazing and delivered more food to us than we knew what to do with. I would put on a happy face when someone came to the door, thank them and chat with them, but then I would go into my bedroom and just surrender to that deep, deep grief. My husband was concerned with how intense my grief was and so he prayed with me, that I would be able to release my dad to God.

"And once I prayed to let him go, I felt the peace come in. When he prayed for me to be able to surrender my dad to Jesus, I was so exhausted. I cried myself to sleep again that night, but I slept deeply. I had a dream of some sort that was peaceful. When I awoke the next morning, I remember there was light coming through the shades and I could hear a bird singing really beautifully. In my spirit, I heard the Lord say, 'My mercies are new every morning.' I had just gone through this hellish night, but when I woke up I felt like I could handle it. It was still really hard, but God provided."

Sometimes grief is like a low fog, slowly rolling over and through your life until it permeates everything without you knowing the extent. Sophie Hudson says, "I've heard so many people say that dementia or Alzheimer's disease feels like a very long goodbye, and I would say that's true. Mama always knew who we were, there wasn't any of the typical memory loss in that sense, but parts of her personality we had known our whole lives changed a little. I did the bulk of grieving Mama's condition in those eighteen months after she was diagnosed, and for a couple years before. Even though she was still here with us, in the weirdest way, I just missed my mama."

Quantrilla Ard was twenty-two and a senior in college when her mother's condition worsened. Processing anticipatory grief proved itself to be difficult for her in that stage of life. "It was really difficult, and I made decisions that I would not have made in a different mindset. I was having a good time and trying to get out of college, but there was a doom and heaviness that always hung over me. I knew I didn't have anywhere else to escape from this horrible thing that was waiting for me at home. I didn't even consider therapy at the time, I just thought, *Everyone has issues or a sick family member.* I didn't realize I was going through a very traumatic experience that isn't typical for college students."

A Word on Guilt

Guilt is an inevitable part of this process. Perhaps you couldn't be there for the first treatment, or able to rush to see your parent as soon as they were diagnosed. Even if it wasn't a logistical issue, but an emotional one that made you keep your distance, I encourage you to offer yourself grace. You did the best you could within the boundaries you had at the time.

Whenever I felt guilt about anything—past arguments, the way I was unable to be there for Mom through previous tragedies—anything at all, Mom would say, "What if it were Bryce or Bradley? Would you want them to carry that? You would forgive them and forget it without a second thought, right?"

She consistently pointed me back to my own mothering journey because she knew that the lens of motherhood's unconditional love would guide me into the space where I let go of my own perceived failings, real or imagined. And just like she knew it would, it worked.

When They Don't Remember You

If your parent has Alzheimer's disease or another form of dementia that impacts memory or their ability to recognize you, guilt may become a familiar companion. Perhaps you find it too difficult to visit often on an emotional level, or even a physical one. In this scenario, you may wonder, *what difference does it make if they don't remember who I am or that I visited?* It's important to maintain as much self-awareness as possible. What will bring you peace after they are gone, or in this present moment? Will you feel guilty for not visiting more, even if they are unaware of your presence? Perhaps you know your parent would want you to carry on with life as usual, and not willingly place any burden or guilt upon your shoulders. It might be helpful to set up a regular visiting schedule or checking in with your parent or their caretaker that feels doable but not overwhelming. Either way, let your future and present peace be your guide.

Balance is an Illusion

Often, we find the way forward as parents by breaking out of the familiar and cyclical parent-child dynamic by putting ourselves in our parent's place instead. We can consider what we would want our children to do for us if the roles were reversed, and how we would feel about their guilt and regret. The balance between supporting and loving our parent through the end of life and devoting ourselves to our family is not much of a balance.

Sometimes our parents will need us, and we must go to them, because we know this is a future regret or sorrow we will carry if we don't. Other times, we will allow someone else to hold their hand while we tend to our children and partners because we know that it will also be a future regret if we don't.

My mother never wanted me to miss out on irreplaceable moments in my own life while she faced the end of hers. If you're unsure of how your parent feels about this, I encourage you to ask them. Simply letting them know you're struggling with guilt about your inability to be two places at once will no doubt be a reflection of the love you have for them.

In the end, we do our best, and it has to be enough. We are only human, and so we give God the rest—a burden only He can bear.

A Moment for Mindfulness

Anticipatory grief can be both helpful and unhelpful, depending on the way it is used, according to Licensed Marriage and Family Therapist and Author, Nicole Zasowski. "Anticipatory grief can be helpful and serves its purpose in the sense that we have time to do the things we are empowered to do, such as expressing the sentiments you haven't expressed to your parent because you think they already know. It allows you to think about how you want to feel when certain milestones or death happens, and what you can do now to ensure that you feel that way. When it spurs you to consider how you're living now in the relationship, it's helpful. What is not helpful is to practice disaster. This is when we think we have a sort of pseudo-control by rehearsing grief. It's the brain's way of trying to prepare you for the worst, believing it will lessen our grieving after the event happens. The research is clear that it doesn't lessen the sting of grief, it only dulls the delight of the present. Anticipatory grief isn't helpful in the future, but it should help steer how you live now."

To stay present in the moment and avoid rehearsing for disaster, Zasowski recommends a practice of thanksgiving. "Joy is one of the most vulnerable feelings, because it's accompanied by the fear of loss. In this scenario, with a terminal parent, you know that you will be experiencing loss. I recommend practicing offering a prayer of thanksgiving to God, because it doubles the joy that we feel. I say thanksgiving and not gratitude, because gratitude helps us to name joy, but thanksgiving is an expression of gratitude to God through prayer. Saying it to God doubles the joy and provides a meaningful experience."

Consider:

- Are you rehearsing for disaster, or allowing anticipatory grief to shape the way you're living now?
- What would your prayer of thanksgiving to God include?

JEN BABAKHAN

A Daughter's Prayer

Father, I know that You have given us tears as a gift to help us process feelings that don't have words. At this time, I don't have the words—just a deep ache that feels endless. Give me the strength to let myself grieve as I need to. I know that You love me and desire only the best for me, Lord. I come to You now asking for a peace that transcends my understanding to settle upon my family and me. Give me the comfort only You can provide. Amen.

SIX

SAY ALL THE THINGS: FINDING PEACE IN THE BEFORE AND AFTER

> If it is possible, as far as it depends on you, be at peace with everyone.
>
> Romans 12:18

I stood next to Mom's hospital bed in the radiology wing while we waited for them to call her back for yet another scan. The room was icy cold, and though I couldn't feel my own hands, I was tucking the dryer-warmed hospital blankets under her feet. "I'm so sorry," I said through tears. "For all the things. All of the fights and disagreements and everything I've ever done. I'm so sorry."

My mother and I often found ourselves at odds on both minor and big things—it was only after her diagnosis that I clearly saw that all of them were minor.

"I'm sorry too. We have bickered like an old married couple, like most moms and daughters," she said, after reassuring me it was all forgiven and forgotten.

In an instant, we had the relationship I yearned for through the years and did not know how to reach. A terminal diagnosis has a way of clearing debris that once blocked a path, a sort of Red Sea moment that simultaneously feels miraculous and heartbreaking.

When my mother was diagnosed with cancer and given six weeks to live that eventually became nearly three years, I instantly wanted to say everything I previously felt too proud to say. Mother-daughter relationships are complex and layered, and those with our fathers can have complexities as well. Apologies for hurts long gone, and expressions of love I hoped she would fully understand regularly peppered our conversations until her passing.

I thought often of Paul's words in Romans advising us, to the extent we are able, to live at peace with everyone. I kept this at the forefront of my mind during conversations with my mom, and all I came into contact with. Never before had I been so conscious of both my words and the brevity of life. I wanted to have no regrets, be quick to forgive, and remember the power of my words.

Several times over the course of the final three years of Mom's life she voiced gratitude for having the chance to make amends where she needed to and say the things that mattered to those that meant the most to her. "Not everyone gets the opportunity," she would say. I knew the importance of voicing what someone means to you before it's too late.

When I was twenty-three, my beloved grandmother and I had a phone call while she was hospitalized that I knew was our last. I recall the sense of feeling as though I needed to tell her how grateful I was for all she had given me in my life, namely, a close relationship with Jesus. She was the first person to tell me to speak to Him as a friend during prayer, instead of trying to craft the perfect words, and it never left my mind or heart. When we hung up, I sat in my bed and cried, the anticipatory grief already visiting in full force. I felt both relieved at saying what I needed to say and pain for all I was losing. There are no easy goodbyes in death, but every goodbye is worth having if God gives you the chance.

About three months before Mom died, her only sister who lived out of state became suddenly ill and hospitalized. Doctors estimated she had days left to live. She was no longer conscious, and my mother agonized that she couldn't talk to her sister in the final moments of life.

"Mom," I said, "why don't you have them hold the phone to her ear? She can still hear you, according to the hospice nurses."

To be honest, I felt helpless and distraught. I knew my mom needed to say goodbye, and I also questioned God's timing. It was unbelievable that we were losing my aunt, who I imagined I would still have after Mom died. We needed Mom to stay strong, though all of us sensed she was nearing her own passing. Later that day, Mom told me she had done what I suggested—she told her sister goodbye and she loved her. I saw peace on her face along with grief.

Her sister was her last remaining immediate family member, and I sensed that after all the pain they had faced as a family, God desired to reunite their family as a whole in heaven. Until Mom was there, she would have the peace of knowing she told her sister she loved her. Sometimes helping our parents find their own words means more than we realize in the moment.

Is there someone your parent needs closure with at this point in their life? If so, is there a way you can facilitate the experience for them, with their permission? Resolving unfinished business is a common desire of those who face their own mortality, and it is a blessing to be able to assist in bringing peace in whatever way you are able.

Peace is Our Goal

Ultimately, whether we are aware of it or not, what we all long for is peace. We want the deepest part of our being, our soul, to find rest in our decisions. Peace isn't happiness, exactly, I would argue it's better than that. To me, peace feels like I am actively within the will of God, and He is pleased with my desire to abide there. When we base our decisions in life with peace as our goal, there is a comfort that comes that is independent of outcomes. A friend's dear late mother-in-law, a beautiful older woman with a delightful southern accent and perfectly applied red lipstick, once advised me to "let peace be my umpire" in life. I took the advice to heart and have consistently found it to be some of the wisest counsel I've received.

As we navigate the unknown with our parent and even within our own heart, following the path that leads to a deep sense of peace can only lead us to the One who *is* peace. We should ask ourselves regularly when making decisions, "Which choice brings me deep and abiding peace at a soul level? What decision feels restful in my spirit? Where do I find myself within God's will?" Paul wrote to the Thessalonians, "Now may the lord of peace himself give you peace at *all times* and in *every way*" (2 Thess. 3:16, emphasis mine).

There is a peace that blankets those who walk with God that covers all situations, in ways we cannot comprehend. Remember, peace is not happiness or a lack of pain, but a true sense of soul rest, knowing that all is well, or *will be* well. The peace that Christ places in our hearts is one that cannot be moved. When we set peace as our goal, we place God at the center of our focus. He is our peace.

Moments that Matter

Mom attended a retreat for cancer patients not long into her treatment journey and returned home glowing. "I got up in front of everyone and I told my story," she said. "And people loved hearing it!"

My father looked so proud. "You should have seen her, she gave a great speech!"

After many years of looking for a purpose outside of her family, it seemed my mother had found hers. Cancer had taken so much from us, but it helped Mom find her voice.

Depending on your unique situation and timetable, your parent may find motivation and encouragement by sharing their story with others. Perhaps they have always wanted to write a book or make a meaningful difference in the lives of others. This may be the time to help your parent find a way to record their thoughts or life story. Ghostwriting services do exactly this. Or your parent may find a support group they can join and share their experience with. Regardless of what motivates them, you can encourage your parent to do something each day that brings them joy.

A Change of Heart

Shay Mason's father was not a Christian, though her mother had tried desperately through the years to change that fact. One afternoon, Shay went to stay with him in the hospital while her mother attended Bible study. "She asked me to come sit with him, which I did most afternoons, but it was typically both of us there with him. I remember Dad was more lucid than he had been, and we talked about his close call with death after a bad reaction to having COVID-19 and his first chemotherapy treatment at the same time. 'That was really scary,' I said. 'Did it frighten you?' And he said, 'Yeah, it's really made me think.' I felt God nudge me to ask him about a relationship with Jesus, and so I did. I told him I knew church had been a struggle and was never his thing, but it wasn't about church. It was about a relationship with Jesus. He wanted to accept Christ, and so I prayed with him.

"We prayed for quite a while, and it was beautiful. My mother had been trying so hard for years for this to happen. Dad didn't say a word about it again until two weeks later, when he was back home, and said he wanted to be baptized. My mom was shocked and looked at me. 'He means it,' I told her. My husband, an Anglican priest, baptized him a week later."

Quantrilla Ard's mother made the most of their final times together. "I think my mom had a lot of regret before she passed away. We tried to squeeze everything into those last few months. We had lots of conversations. I wasn't aware how short the time together was, but she knew. I'm an only child, so she hit me with a lot of hard stuff—a lot of history between her and my father, and her and the Lord. There were lots of conversations that I think she wanted to have with me all along, but she knew I wasn't ready or I was resistant. I was both of those things. Anytime she tried to talk to me about something, I'd say I just couldn't hear it. It was my own selfishness, to keep it from being real. It wasn't for the lack of trying because she knew her time was short.

"We literally talked almost those entire two months. She told me everything—laid her life bare. I don't know if I could have absorbed more in those moments or not, but she finally had my attention. There was anticipatory grief hanging over every conversation. I just thought there was going to be more time. There was a point that she asked me to anoint her. It was surreal, and I kept thinking, *I'm not an elder or a pastor*. And she said, 'You don't need to be.' That was a seed she was planting from then, that you don't need anyone else to come alongside your healing. God has given you healing power. I anointed her. I was in awe that she trusted me to do this thing for her and pray for her healing. Even though the prayer wasn't answered the way we wanted, it was ultimately answered."

For some, finding the words to bridge a divide or make up for past hurts won't come easily. Too much has been said or done, and it all feels too heavy to overcome. In this case, writing a letter to your parent may feel more fitting for your processing of the details, even if you can't find the courage just yet, or ever, to deliver it.

Mary Boswell's mother took a few moments to go through her jewelry box with Mary and her sister. "It was important for her to go through her jewelry. She gave us the history of some of her pieces and where they came from. I now have a pair of earrings that were from my grandfather, who gave them to her mother. They're made of Argentinian gold he got when he worked the pipelines long ago. Hearing those stories, and her view of different things was important to her. For me, it was such a blessing to be with her and caring for her in those final days. That's what was important to my heart and meant more than anything. I wanted to be able to be there to help her put on her clothes and wheel her in her wheelchair into the den so we could sit and talk together. I called those 'bedside blessings,' because it was a blessing for me to get to care for her in her last days."

After They're Gone

Not all of us make it to the bedside of our parent in time to say our final words, or have an opportunity to broach difficult topics while they're still alive. I don't believe feeling guilty is a response that your parent or God would choose for you in this moment. Perhaps there is a way to channel your feelings of guilt into something meaningful and productive, such as honoring your parent by delivering a eulogy, or writing their obituary.

I remember the moment my mother asked me to deliver her eulogy. "I know it will be hard. Think of it as a gift to me," she said.

When she put it that way, as a final gift I could offer, I was determined to deliver her eulogy well. I believe she knew it would be cathartic and healing for me to share both my joy of having her as a mother, and my deep pain in losing her as a grandmother to my boys with others.

I stood before a small group of family because of COVID-19 restrictions in front of her grave, and said the words I knew would honor my mom best. I cried through the segment about my boys, and struggled to maintain my composure, but I did it. I gave Mom the gift she requested.

While I spoke, groups of small yellow butterflies fluttered through the gravesite, as though she herself was floating through. It was a beautiful and gut-wrenching day, unlike any I had experienced before. It was purely God's strength alone carrying me, as I watched my boys stare numbly at her coffin, and later, as I watched it be settled into the ground. Even now, the reality of the funeral feels like too much to truly take in, so surreal and piercingly painful at once.

The Unexplainable

Before she died, I asked my mom to leave us signs after her death if she was still with us in some way or aware of our lives, and she responded, "I'll do as much as God allows me. Maybe I'll visit as a hummingbird!" Her submission to His will for her both in life and death was profound.

Since Mom has passed, countless experiences have cemented for each of us in our family that she is somehow, in some way, still aware of our lives, even from heaven. I won't share all of them, but a couple still leave me a bit breathless and bolster my faith.

A few months after she died, my son was having a difficult time before bed. He was inconsolable over the loss of his grandma. *Mom, we need a sign from you to get us through this pain,* I thought. I went to bed that night desperate to feel close to her again somehow. During the first couple of years after her death, it was often in the darkness before bed when the full weight of her loss sat on my chest. I awoke the next morning as usual, blissfully forgetting the previous night's desperate prayers and emotions. Making my way around our breakfast nook, I opened each of the kitchen blinds.

When I opened the final blind above our kitchen sink, a hummingbird hovered in front of the window. Our eyes locked. It hovered in place for about ten seconds, and I stared back in disbelief, speechless. As I gazed into its eyes, I felt a sweet connection and delighted at this tiny bird, hovering a good morning "hello." It buzzed away after it made its point, and it was then I remembered my thoughts from the night before. *Mom we need a sign.*

When the boys awoke, I shared the experience with them, and they were ecstatic. We all needed this moment of assurance. It was enough to carry us through when we were feeling her loss so acutely.

About six months after Mom died, I had a dream of her that I knew in every cell of my body was a message from her to me. In the dream, my family was gathering for my brother's birthday. When my father walked through the door, my mother stood next to him, but was invisible to all but me. She winked at me and smiled, and I stared at her, dumbfounded. She was there throughout the party, until at one point, she disappeared in front of my eyes.

I knew that it was my mother's way of letting me know she was watching over us, especially during the milestone events when we so dearly missed her presence. After that dream I remembered her telling me that she would be with us in some way— we just wouldn't see her, after she passed. Perhaps she felt the same closeness to her mother after she died, proving to her that the division between heaven and earth is simply a thin veil. I don't claim to know how it works, and what God allows and doesn't, but I have felt such comfort when I feel these supernatural hugs.

A friend from junior high school was always close with my mom— to the point that she called her "Other Mom" or "O.M." for short. She and I speak from time to time, but I hadn't yet shared with her about this book I planned to write about the loss of a parent. She sent me a text message that said she had a dream of my mom, and she just *knew* it was really her spirit with her in the dream. I was so intrigued to hear what it could have been about. She said, "In the dream your mom handed me a book, and she said it was the first draft. She said it was about her life and that it would help people. Then, she said she was giving it to you, because you were in charge of it now."

Too stunned to know how to respond, I stared at her messages. When I told her about this book, she was speechless as well. Later that day, the details of the dream still rolling around in my mind, it occurred to me that my mother—and God—would choose to have a friend reveal the dream to me instead of me experiencing it myself.

I have had multiple dreams of my mother that answered some questions I've had, and I know they were her spirit with me in them. This dream, however, would have made me second-guess its validity. Of course, I would dream about the book if I had just signed a contract to write it, why *wouldn't* my brain make up a dream about my mom and the book. This dream not only confirmed my deep spirit sense that I was to write this book, but also strengthened my friend's faith that our mothers (her mother had passed as well) were still present in some way in our lives.

Shay Mason had an experience that felt like a hug from God and her earthly father too. "My mom and I were on our way to pick up my dad's ashes, and I asked her how she was doing. She said music had become an emotional trigger for her, and hearing love songs or any emotional songs would really set her off. We were listening to a mix station that played anything from the sixties onward. We were singing along with Lionel Richie, and then the next song that came on was my mom and dad's song. It's a fairly obscure song, and we were minutes from picking up his ashes.

"Mom asked, 'What are the odds of that? Do you think he can communicate?' I told her I didn't have all the answers, but God knew that song would come on and mean something to you. Maybe the angels delivered a message to have that song played. I don't know, but that song was for you. Not long after, Shay had a dream that felt like confirmation of her dad's happiness. My dad loved to grill, and in this dream I was standing on our patio and looking at our neighbor's patio, who are a lovely Christian couple. In the dream, my dad was standing on their patio grilling, but on the other side of a fence. I couldn't get to him. I saw him and I waved, and he looked up, nodded at me, and kept grilling. I felt like, *oh, he's really happy*. He's doing what he loves. It felt like my dad was in the right place."

God is kind to us in our grief. He alone knows what we will need before and after such profound loss. It's why there will be moments for those of us walking closely with the Lord that make us say, "Only God could have known what this would mean." What is difficult for us to comprehend is crystalline clarity to the Father. His ways are not our own, and He is and will be merciful in ways we cannot predict.

While we count down the weeks and months left with our parent, or how long it's been since they passed, there is no scarcity of time for God. Imagine for a moment the conversations we will have when we are once again face to face with our parent and other loved ones. When the veil is lifted, and there are no questions about how communication works between heaven and earth. Reunited again, never to part. With God, there is always more. More grace, more love, more abundance, more time—eternity—with our loved ones to be shared. What a gift He's given us and continues to offer. Life—true life—is endless.

A Moment for Mindfulness

According to Clinical Psychologist Barbara Greenberg, PhD, speaking grief and experiential narratives out loud makes a difference in the way the brain processes. "People are much less likely to have post-traumatic stress disorder (PTSD) if they form a narrative and talk out loud. The brain processes it differently if you form a story, and you're less likely to have trauma, if for example, you see someone later that looks like your mother or father in the grocery store after they've passed. In the Jewish faith mourning tradition, we sit Shiva, which includes the telling of stories about the loved one who is now gone. Telling people and talking about it helps you to make sense of the loss."

Consider:

- Who can you share your story out loud with?
- What are the main details you would like to share to help lighten your heart?
- Is there someone who knew your parent who might have a story to share with you?

A Daughter's Prayer

God, You care about me in ways I cannot fathom. You give me opportunities for healing and comfort that know no bounds. I ask that You would continue to provide moments for me to express myself that will bring peace to me in this hard journey I am walking. I don't understand how communication works on Your side of heaven, Father. I am grateful for the moments of comfort You provide me with when I need them the most. Please continue to give me eyes to see all the beautiful ways You are at work in my life every day. Amen.

SEVEN

KEEP SOME AIR FOR YOURSELF: WHY SAVING ROOM FOR NORMAL IS NON-NEGOTIABLE

> If any of you lacks wisdom, you should ask God, who gives generously to all without finding fault, and it will be given to you.
>
> James 1:5

A light breeze twirled around us as the scent of popcorn and churros reminded us it was time for lunch. Disneyland was a delightful diversion from the clinical trial statistics and the nagging anxiety settling in my stomach while I waited to hear Mom's latest scan results.

Finally, in between rides, I could wait no more. I pulled to the side of the path filled with strollers and exhausted parents, and dialed Mom's cell phone, knowing she had probably met with her doctor by then and knew the results of the scan. I tried to sound calm and like I didn't feel nauseated when she answered. After some small talk about our trip, I asked. "What did they say?" "Well, it's working!" she replied, her voice full of hope. "The tumors are all shrinking. The doctor is happy. We just stay the course for now."

My stomach settled again, and my appetite returned. I ended the call, rejoined the rest of my family, and gave them the good news. We nearly skipped that Disneyland trip. It hadn't felt right to leave knowing Mom would be getting results while we were gone.

I wondered what if the results were bad. Would it ruin our trip? Yet I knew that we had to go. More than that, we *needed* to. My boys had needed the respite as much as I did. We needed a few days to embrace joy and laughter and food shaped like mouse ears.

I spent the rest of the trip in relieved joy, it felt like a deep exhale after holding my breath. The thought that one day I would get a call that wouldn't be a relief niggled the back of my mind, but I blocked it out. We weren't in that place yet, and we embraced good news and carefree fun while we could.

I was learning, slowly but surely, on this journey that one of the biggest and most valuable lessons this experience would teach was the value of staying in the present moment, and training my mind to neither flash forward or backward. For someone with anxiety, like me, this was difficult and a constant struggle.

The Importance of a True Break

Maintaining your typical schedule is important for your mental health. It is also vital to allow yourself to have a reprieve from your new reality of tests and treatment, or care at home.

The metaphor of putting your oxygen mask on first before placing it onto your child during a flight is apt here. We cannot give what we don't have. If your other parent is the caregiver, I cannot stress the importance enough of providing them time to live their lives as normally as possible when you can. Some hospice programs will offer "respite care" for the caregiving spouse. This is a wonderful option if you or your siblings cannot offer it yourself. My mother encouraged my father to go visit other relatives or take a break whenever he could, especially when she was receiving treatment and feeling stable but tired.

Not only does continuing with life as best as you can keep your own family's life humming, it also signals to your parent that you will be okay without them. For most parents this is a fear that looms large over his or her prognosis: *How will everyone handle life after I'm gone? Are they strong enough to lose me and be okay? Will they take care of each other?*

As a parent this would be my biggest fear as well, and I think it's a common one. We just want our children to thrive, even if we aren't here—*especially* if we aren't here.

I continued my daily workout routine—which in truth, helped me keep my anxiety and mental health under control—homeschooled my children, and tried to keep life normal for my boys wherever I could.

During treatment weeks, I would make dinner for my parents, even if it was just frozen lasagna. It helped me to feel as though I were doing something helpful in a helpless feeling time. I also kept their dog at my house as they made the drive to doctor appointments in the Bay Area. I wanted to help in every way I could, knowing it would help me to continue to feel at peace as much as possible.

The Opinions of Others

Throughout this journey, you may find that others have lots of *big feelings*, like you do, about the health and prognosis of your parent. They may also have *big opinions* about the treatments they believe your parent should or shouldn't try, including all sorts of anecdotes of what worked for their friend or someone they saw on the Internet. I've often found that these are also the people who may overlook any sort of empathy for what you are enduring, as the *child* of a very ill parent, and focus instead on how the impending loss affects them.

These are the people who have a bit more nerve than others—you know the ones. Perhaps they are just *devastated* about your parent, on a day you felt like your grief was finally giving you a break. If you're having a hard day, suddenly it becomes about all the things that have gone wrong in *their* day. Maybe they feel the need to remind you that you should get yourself checked for the same condition your parent has or that you should begin a new supplement they've read will prevent it. These are bold examples, but unfortunately I have a feeling they aren't unrealistic.

Make sure you stay aware of how much you allow their words or tone to affect you, and actively take it to God. Ask Him to help you find peace again and heal any wounds their words created. Also, take note of how you feel emotionally and physically when they speak with you, and after they leave. You may find it helpful to go for a long walk, or talk to an understanding friend, to rid yourself of the discomfort they often leave in their wake.

While these types of people mean well, and we can give the benefit of the doubt where it is due, I encourage you to only give them the space and time you think they deserve in your family's life and *no more* than that. When there is limited time left, your family has every right to be choosey about who and what kind of energy comes in and out of your sacred home space.

I think of the way Jesus only took His closest disciples into the room with Him to heal the little girl in the book of Mark. He was very specific about those He chose to be present. "He did not let anyone follow Him except Peter, James, and John the brother of James... After He put them all out, He took the child's father and mother and the disciples who were with him, and went in where the child was" (Matt. 5:37-40). There are times when it is appropriate that only the closest family or friends are present, and I would argue that as your parent progresses, this will be the majority of the time.

A Word on Complex Emotions

It's important to note that during this time you may begin to feel a bit more isolated than usual because of the circumstances. After the initial diagnosis, much like after the funeral, people who once sent cards, casseroles, and condolences, go back to living their lives. It's expected, and even natural for this to happen, yet for the adult child still handling details of care while trying to also maintain a level of pre-diagnosis normalcy, this time can feel lonely. Allowing yourself to acknowledge the emotions this brings up is a healthy step in processing them.

This is also true if you find yourself feeling jealous toward those whose mothers or fathers aren't suffering side effects or symptoms of illness, especially on holidays when people tend to post their celebratory photos online. On social media, not only does everyone have picture-perfect relationships with their parents, but they also seem untouched by the gritty difficulties of life, like severe memory loss, chemotherapy, and pill schedules.

This is a lie, of course, but in the moment the lie feels true. I would encourage you to remind yourself of the truth—that everyone has difficulty in life, and the realities you now face will eventually become realities for others. Still, it's okay to wish it wasn't true, right now, for your family.

Social Media Self-Care

This is also applicable after your parent has died. Holidays such as Mother's or Father's Day can be painful, especially if you're on social media. It might be an act of self-care to log off all social media on difficult days. It is helpful to take this pain to God through real and honest prayer during these moments when it feels as though others have what you want, or don't seem "grateful" enough for their healthy or living parent. He knows intimately what your family is experiencing and will be faithful to provide you with the insight and strength your heart needs.

If you have siblings, it's ideal to try and work together so that no one person bears the responsibility alone, although I understand this isn't an option for every family with multiple adult children. If not, perhaps a family friend could bridge the gap for you when needed, even if it isn't a regular occurrence.

My brother and I took turns doing what we could for both of our parents and compared notes often to plan for the coming days. I often told him during Mom's illness that I was so grateful for him, and it was the absolute truth. He took the brunt of attending appointments or staying at the hospital with Mom so I could be home with my boys at night, and it meant so much.

Sophie Hudson's siblings shared her mother's care as well. "My brother, sister, and I all lived out of town, so I felt some guilt as a result. My sister had the most flexibility with her work and was able to go be with Mama for a week or two at a time. The summer before she was diagnosed, I was able to spend more time there, but one thing we all did was to check in with Daddy and make sure he was good."

If you're not living close enough to your parent to make quick visits and drop meals by, it's easy to let guilt settle in. In those moments, it's vital you remind yourself that your parent would most likely rather you continue to thrive in your life wherever that is than to drop everything if it will create a burden for yourself. This is certainly true when your parent suffers from a long-term diagnosis such as dementia, lung disease, or heart failure.

A Caveat

However, if you feel burdened in your spirit, or have a gut instinct to be with your parent, it's a good idea to pay close attention to that stirring. I've learned in life these instinctual and spiritual nudges are often the whisper of the Holy Spirit. We don't have to know why they are there at the moment, only that they serve a purpose. Pay attention to how your body feels when you consider your plans. Let peace be the guiding factor, even if it doesn't make sense at the time. Ask yourself, *what will bring me the most peace when they are gone? Will I regret this choice?* You can trust God—ask Him too. He will be faithful to answer in some way.

The Balancing Act

When the woman or man who has led us through life receives a startling diagnosis, our first instinct is often to rearrange our lives to be with them as much as we can. For the first weeks or even months after their diagnosis, this is expected and even encouraged. After a time, usually when treatment has begun and things for the moment are more stable, it is healthy to try and return to as normal a life as you can, for your children and family's sake. There is nothing gained in losing your joy. Your family and children need you at your best, or the closest you can get to it.

My mother modeled this well for my brother and me when her best friend, Theresa, was dying of cancer. Theresa had two young children at the time, and though my mother's heart was absolutely broken at the process of losing her dear friend, she never hesitated to walk toward the pain and difficult moments, and then return and be present with us.

When Theresa died, our phone rang in the middle of the night. Her children asked if my mother would come hold them. I heard the garage door open, and my mother left to go comfort her best friend's children.

I wasn't a mother then, but I knew I was witnessing something sacred—a true act of love and friendship. It struck me later that when she was with Theresa and her children, she was fully present with them, and when she came home to us, she was present with us. We saw her grieve, but we also witnessed the gratitude and presence she held for her own family at home.

Sometimes life happens differently than you expect, even amid an already unexpected time. For Quantrilla Ard, working to gain a sense of balance during her mother's illness meant going back to college for one more class so she could officially graduate. "The college gave me a provisional graduation that meant I still had to complete one class I took and didn't pass once I got home. Taking this class gave me a sense of normalcy, it felt like I was back in my everyday life. I thought, *I'm going to finish this class and as soon as I do, everything will be fine.* It was an outlet for me until it wasn't. In the middle of this course my mom passed away, right as I was studying for a test. That sense of normalcy got shattered immediately, and I still had work to do and turn in. I had to finish the class, but my mom was gone."

Shay Mason was supposed to leave for Scotland the day after she learned her father had pancreatic cancer. "My parents had been planning to go to Scotland with us for Thanksgiving to see my daughter who was in college there. My dad wasn't feeling up to it before he was diagnosed, so they cancelled their plans. They told us what the doctors had found the night before we were to leave. It hit me like a wall, but the Lord was so present at the same time. I always imagined I would be undone with that kind of news, but there was strength instead. God was sustaining us. We cried and prayed with my father, who was not a believer at that time, but welcomed prayer. We went to Scotland, and it was good. We felt like we were missing my parents. We tried to make the best of it, but it was hard."

Living in the liminal space of having a terminally ill parent while continuing to live a life that feels true to yourself is an exercise in duality. Done well, it further provides you with the energy necessary to be what your parent needs. It will require that you know what fills you, what inspires you, and what gives you more energy than it takes.

The day my mother was diagnosed, I came home from the hospital that night exhausted and drained. Nothing felt right. And I remembered a deadline I had to meet the next morning for a freelance project. I certainly could have sent a note to my editor and got an extension without any trouble, but something about sitting back at my desk—untouched since my world flipped upside down—was comforting to me.

That night I sat and typed, forcing all traumatic memories from the day to the side. I had one focus, and I would not be deterred. I finished the article and, feeling accomplished, sent it on time. It was the first moment in that awful and shocking day when I sensed that life would go on in some way, even if it wasn't the same life as before. Every single thing in my life didn't have to change. It wasn't either/or, it was both/and. Enjoyment and anxiety could exist at once. Laughter and tears sometimes arrived in the same minute. Life isn't black and white. There's a whole lot of grey when you have eyes to see it.

The week my mother died, I needed to finish another writing project. This one required I conduct an interview. Again, I could either give the project up, or face it head on. There was a split second when I decided to complete it that I felt guilty. Was I really going to conduct a phone interview from my parent's home while my mom was in her last days? Even as I reflected on it, I instinctively questioned my decision. And then I remembered how much I *needed* to do something during those days when time felt both endless and scarce in the same breath.

My writing saved me. It always had, since I was an eight-year-old with her first diary—with a lock on it, thank you very much. I wasn't running from the grief of losing my mom. Well, maybe I was, a little. I knew what I needed, and it was to do the one thing that brought me joy during so much anguish.

I knew my mom would have told me to do exactly what I did. After all, she was the first and consistent voice in my life insisting that writing was my calling. I denied it for a long time, but like most things, moms just *know*.

Unexpected Comforts

Sometimes, the thing you feel called to do will be the very thing that brings comfort to your parent when they need it most—I believe God loves when that happens. Sophie Hudson found a few things that brought her and her mother comfort during the difficult moments in her life with dementia. "There were things about Mama that never changed, even if her disposition was a little bit different. Up until the end, if she could have, she would have put on her makeup and an outfit to go to the hospital. She never stopped going to her bedroom two hours before bedtime so she could roll her hair.

"These things were so deeply ingrained in her. When I would go home to help or give Daddy a break, I would do for her what she had always done for us. I would make her big pots of potato soup—her favorite. She loved to wake up and have her coffee and toast with copious amounts of apple butter. I did those kinds of things for her. This was also the strangest thing, but it brought me comfort that the very first book I wrote was about her family. So many times when I would go home, I would go check on her after she'd gotten in bed, and she would be reading that book because those were memories. More than anything, I'm so glad I did that. It's not the fact that I wrote a book, but because it was a comfort to my mama when she was struggling. It comforted her in a different way than me asking to tell her a story about her family. It felt familiar to her. What brought us comfort was trying to figure out how we could love her like she loved us."

Perhaps the best example we have of Jesus taking a moment for Himself in a time of great sorrow and strain is revealed in the book of Matthew, after he receives news that John the Baptist has been beheaded. It says, "When Jesus heard what had happened, he withdrew by boat privately to a solitary place. Hearing of this, the crowds followed Him on foot from the towns. When Jesus landed and saw a large crowd, He had compassion on them and healed their sick" (Matt. 14:13-14).

Jesus's response was to remove Himself from the crowd and presumably spend time with the Father. We get the sense that the news of His beloved cousin being murdered, and in such a brutal way, brought deep pain to Jesus. He pulled away to a solitary place. He knew what He required in that moment, and then He allowed Himself to have it.

We should note what happened after His time away—He performed the miracle of feeding five thousand people with five loaves of bread and two fish. His time away did not change who He was, or His mission. He returned to it with enthusiasm.

And so do we, after providing ourselves with what we need in the moment. No shame. No guilt. We are *not* stronger than the Savior of the world. So, we can rest when we need to too.

A Moment for Mindfulness

Though it's tempting to give in to the struggle to be everything and everywhere for everyone, Licensed Marriage and Family Therapist and Author, Nicole Zasowski, advises against it. "Be where you are. There is a world where you can always feel as though you should be somewhere that you're not. If you're with your parent, you'll feel guilt for missing a day of your children's childhood—or you can fully be where you are. There is always a both/and, but you can feel the freedom to connect with where your feet are. Anxiety will try to pull you into the future and ask 'what if' or to the past and say, 'would've, could've, should've.' One way to really savor the moment and be where you are, is to ask your five senses what they're going to remember about this present moment. Savoring helps us to stay present."

Consider:

- How can you remind yourself to be where you are? Perhaps placing a small note where you can see it when you're feeling anxious may be helpful.

- How can you savor the moments you hope to remember in a meaningful way while you're living them?

A Daughter's Prayer

Lord, You know my exhaustion—both emotional and physical—runs deep. I struggle to be all the things I feel called to be, and balancing my own needs feels difficult. I ask that You would remind me when I have forgotten, that there is time to rest. Please show me when I need to take a step back to replenish so I can serve my family more effectively. Help me to remember what brings me joy, even in the middle of all this sorrow and uncertainty. Thank you for listening to my prayers when I struggle with jealousy, and it seems as though others still have what I used to. Remind me daily that the joy of You, the Lord, is my strength. Thank you for being with me always. Amen.

EIGHT
THE EYE OF THE STORM
WITNESSING THE WORST
AND PROCESSING THE SURREAL
REALITY OF DEATH

> But He said to me, "My grace is sufficient for you, for my power is made perfect in weakness."
>
> 2 Corinthians 12:9

I knew at my son Bryce's seventh birthday. Mom looked different, though I could not put my finger on what exactly it was. Apparently, death, when it sets its sights on someone, has a certain look. Her eyes, seemingly lighter in color, both focused on me and looked through me at the same time. She was losing even more weight, and her face resembled others I had seen nearing the end.

Those faces were always other mothers and fathers, though, never my own. It was a startling realization—the very moments I feared a couple years earlier in a hospital breezeway were coming to pass. She wasn't merely a terminal patient any longer. She was dying, and she looked like it now.

Another five months passed for it to become official. For the doctors to let us know that not only was her cancer treatment ineffective, but the heart murmur she had since birth was now causing heart failure.

I was browning ground beef for tacos the evening she called. She was still at the hospital after her appointment where doctors noticed she had trouble breathing during a routine test. With resignation and peace drifting through her words, she said, "I'm going on hospice, Jen. There's no more to do, and I'm tired. I want to enjoy the time I have left at home."

"Okay. That makes sense," I said. The information was not shocking. I can't even say I was surprised. I knew in my gut that this would be her last trip to the hospital for scans and results. I knew she was done. In truth, we all were.

The Difficult Descent

One of the greatest pains I've experienced is watching my beloved mother decline and ultimately die. It is a sorrow that often lacks vocabulary to describe. In the month prior to her death, my family contracted an illness unlike any we had ever experienced, only later learning of the new COVID-19 virus and presuming that was what we endured.

While we were sick, we maintained our distance. I wasn't aware of how much Mom was declining, even though I could hear her voice weakening and confusion settling in during a few of our conversations.

When I was well enough to see her again, reality was a brisk slap to the face. Her body was horribly jaundiced, and her consciousness came and went. I knew then that I had to bring my boys to visit one last time before it would become too much for their little minds to understand. Even then, during our last visit, she wasn't the same Grandma they remembered.

I was on the elliptical machine, doing my daily workout, when my father called. Exercise had become the way I tried to burn off the extra anxiety that kept me tossing and turning each night, waking me promptly at three in the morning to pray and prepare myself for the inevitable pain I knew we would soon face on a new level.

"The nurses say it's getting close, she's showing some signs that it's near."

My stomach dropped and my feet slowed to a stop. Sweating and breathless, I got off the phone and told Ed, "I have to go now. It's close."

A look of understanding and sorrow crossed his face when I went upstairs to change.

In that moment, I didn't know what "close" meant. When I arrived at the house, I found Mom sleeping deeply. She didn't stir when I walked to her chair to look at her. The thing about dying is this: It's a mystery. No one can tell you how fast or slow it will go. I called the hospice line to get more information.

"It really depends," the nurse on the other line said. "She can go on like this for weeks, but once she stops eating, then it's a lot closer."

I remembered Ed telling me about his father's death rattle, and how haunting the sound was.

"Is there any chance we will skip over that part? Do some people just not do that?" I asked the nurse.

"Rarely, but it does happen. There's a specific way the body shuts down, and most of the time it happens," she said.

Resignation settled in my gut. We were going to have to endure this. My childhood fears and anxiety bubbled to the surface of my mind. *What if I have a panic attack right as she's taking her last breath, and I miss it? What if I'm not strong enough for this? What if I simply cannot bear to do this?* I wondered each night as anxiety woke me from sleep, my pulse and mind racing to find a way to side-step the tsunami that would wash away my sense of normalcy, my family as we knew it, my *mom*. I was thirty-nine, but I felt like a child. Losing a parent has a way of doing that.

The Thinning Veil

My brother and I spent the week at my parents' home, each of us taking turns going to our own homes to do what was needed. My boys hated that I was gone so much, and wanted her to get better.

One night, while I lay next to her, listening to her rhythmic raspy breath, she talked in her sleep. At first, I believed it was a simple dream, but it shortly became clear it was not—it was a visit. She was speaking to my grandmother and her sister, both invisible to me. She talked about her father who was also apparently there, and I got the feeling her brothers also were present. Her entire immediate family was speaking to her there in the living room.

I stared into the space in front of her, willing myself to be able to see them too. It seemed as though in whatever way they appeared to her, they were no different than they had been when they were here on earth. There was no shock or excitement, it was as though they were picking up with her where they left off a long time ago.

In that moment I knew they were coming to take her home, but she wasn't ready just yet. She told them out loud she couldn't go, and she stopped talking.

A month earlier, she told me she dreamed her family was together again in a car and traveling somewhere. "I don't know where we were going, but we were so happy."

This seemed to be different, and not a dream at all. She nodded and responded to my grandmother's inaudible voice in the same way she had when I would listen to them talk late into the evening as a child. This was no different. Her mother was there, and I yearned to see what my mom saw.

The following day, Mom regained consciousness for longer than a few minutes. She stared at each of us intently and told us she loved us. And then she said, "You have to let me go."

I realized she had been holding on for us. She sensed that each of us was struggling so deeply, but her body was so tired of holding on. We reassured her she was free to go, and of our love for her, but I knew she saw through it. A mother's heart will always fight to stay with her family.

That evening, she ate for the first time in days, doing what the hospice nurse told us they called "rallying," when the dying suddenly regain energy and become lucid, right before they progress to the final stages of their transition into eternity. We knew what it was, but it felt like a little bit of magic—to have her back with us in that way, if only for a little while.

That night was a restless one for all of us, Mom couldn't find a comfortable position to lie in, and I silently wondered how long her suffering

DISRUPTED

would continue. Repeatedly throughout the week I couldn't help but mentally compare the process of dying with the process of birth. Both required so much of the body and soul, an endless and rhythmic work to bring forth life. Birth brings new life into this world, and death carries the spirit into eternity, where life really begins.

Pain and joy accompany both. The word "transition" is used in birth to signify a shift into active labor, and in death to signify the final steps into new life. Family gathers, in birth around a bed, and in death as well. The moments felt both holy and utterly ordinary.

Life was typical for everyone else outside our door, but within the four walls of my parent's home, my mother was dying. It was beyond my comprehension. Death was truly a part of life, and I struggled to reconcile how ordinary and extraordinary it felt at once.

Earlier that day, a nurse insisted we move Mom to the hospital bed in one of the bedrooms because it would be easier after she passed for everyone involved, specifically those tasked with removing her body. It was such a foreign concept to me, to speak of such a thing in front of the dying, and yet for the nurse this was her life's work and a fact of life, like adding two plus two to get four, or mixing blue and yellow to make green.

We moved Mom to the bed, and I struggled to watch her grimace with every move while they eased her head against the pillow. In the weeks before, I gave her massages to try and ease some of the aching and body pain, but touch had grown too painful as she progressed.

I had a deep sense that moving her into the bed—her actual "death bed"— would give her the permission she needed to leave us. That night, we heard the start of the dreaded death rattle, just as awful as I anticipated it would be. We knew her transition to heaven was close. We tried to stay awake through the night, sitting in chairs around her bed, though I failed that attempt miserably.

At one point, my brother woke me up. I had been using her feet as a pillow unknowingly and passed out in a deep sleep. *Mom would be heartbroken at the sight of me asleep on her feet*, I thought, but it was the truest illustration of my desperation to be near her for as long as I could.

After I woke up, I read scripture aloud, and my brother sang her one of her favorite songs while he played guitar. We were walking her home the best way we knew how, our little family of four, soon to be three—a sort of birth in reverse, trying to prepare to lose part of our hearts.

A Beautiful Day

We awoke to the most beautiful day I've ever seen. The sky was a bright blue, dotted with huge fluffy clouds. The sun shone brightly, and a gentle breeze rustled the trees outside Mom's window, abloom with beautiful purple blossoms. A huge blue jay—the brightest shade of blue I've seen on a bird of that type, sat upon the fence in the backyard. I stared at it in wonder. My father had also seen it and rushed to get his camera. The day was too beautiful to be the worst of my life.

My brother and I took turns administering her medication and moistening her lips with the tiny sponges that hospice left us. It was both emotionally numbing and achingly slow.

Mom had fallen into a comatose state and was no longer conscious. When the nurse came to assess Mom the next day, next to her bed, I asked the question no one can answer but God. "How long do you think she has at this point?"

"Oh it could be another week, maybe," the nurse said.

"I sure hope for her sake it's sooner," I said. "I never thought I'd get to that point, but I just hate to see her suffer." Looking back, I know that this was what Mom needed to hear from me to fully let go. She was waiting to hear those words that it was okay. We wanted her released to God, free of pain.

Four hours later, with all of us around her bedside, I held my mother's hand, and she ran into the arms of Jesus. I watched as her pulse slowed to a stop, the silence in the room deafening.

She was gone. It was over.

I didn't panic like I worried I would, because God gave me both strength and peace in those days I never could have predicted. Death had not been peaceful as most people would later ask—a birth into new life rarely is. It proved itself to be painful and slow, an act of hard work that required every ounce of energy from everyone involved. The very end—that was peaceful, much like after a baby is born, and the chaos of labor quiets only to the soft whimper of an infant.

A Last Breath Sermon

For Sophie Hudson, her mother's death proved to be an experience that strengthened her faith in ways she couldn't have imagined. "Being with my mama when she died has been more of a comfort to me than anything. I've gone back to that experience over and over because of what happened with her. Mama had a massive stroke and was completely paralyzed on her left side. When I went to visit her in the hospital, her head was resting all the way down on her shoulder. She didn't move, that entire time she was in the hospital room, and she looked like she was having a very hard time. We learned later that she had a massive stroke and there was no brain activity except for her brain stem. The neurologist told us we would most likely lose her that day. My brother, sister, and cousin, who was really close to my mother, and I went back to her room. We had been there for several hours and the machine that regulated her oxygen and pulse began beeping. My cousin said, 'She's not breathing.' I jumped up and we all stood in stillness around her bed. The machine continued to beep, and we could see she had stopped breathing.

"And then—it was the most surreal thing. Her head began to come up, from its resting place down on her shoulder, slow and straight. My brother said, 'She's moving.' We watched her head come up and up, until it was straight up. Her face looked as if thirty years had been wiped away. All the features of her face that were drawn went back to their original place. When we left the room to let those in the waiting room know she was gone, one of my sister's friends said, 'You look like someone who's been in the presence of Jesus.' I grabbed my son's face and said, 'We're going to be sad, but we can be so happy for her.'

"That night I couldn't stop thinking about it. I couldn't sleep. I tried researching on the Internet to see whether this was a normal occurrence for stroke victims—there was nothing on such a thing. I told my friend, a Bible teacher, about it. 'I need you to know what we saw.' She said, 'I need you to know that you saw Jesus take your mama home.' I don't know why we got to have that experience except for the kindness of God. The next day my brother said it was a miracle.

"When we came into the room and saw her looking so unlike herself, our only hope was that she would be whole and free once again. And for us to get to see her body look whole again in our presence was just *remarkable*. The reason it brings me so much comfort is because I think my mama— with her very last breath that she ever took, preached a whole sermon to her children. It reminds me of what she did so beautifully my entire life: She was present. She was not a helicopter mom, but she was present. She was present in her family's life, she was present with us, and she was present with the Lord. When I think about the end of her life, I'm so comforted that her final testimony was, *it's all true*. It was the strangest, most unexpected joy, in the middle of something that was heartbreaking."

She Won the Race

Jaime Jo Wright's mother surprised everyone with her passing. "The night before she died, my sister-in-law and my husband stayed the night with my parents. I was sick with an infection, but by the next morning I was well enough to go be with her. We were told she had begun the dying process, but she wasn't suffering. She really seemed as though she had the stomach flu, and just felt a little under the weather. Hospice came later that morning to deliver her hospital bed, and over the course of several hours she decided she did want to get in bed, but not the hospital bed—her own. I sat in the chair in the corner of her bedroom, and we cracked some jokes. Then, she pointed to something and said, 'I want you to have that.' And then she continued pointing out other things, very much aware and conscious.

"She was getting ready to fall asleep, when my husband told her he was leaving to pick up our kids from school. 'You take a nap, and hopefully I'll be back by the time you wake up,' he said. 'Well, I'll race you,' she replied. 'I'll beat you,' he said. 'No, I'll beat you,' she said. It was their typical banter back and forth. He left, and about five minutes later, mom asked me to turn up her oxygen. I let her know I needed to check about that, because at a certain point we had to call a nurse. As I was leaving the room, she got a strange look on her face. I went to get my sister-in-law and said, 'I don't think everything is alright.'

"She went in and looked at her and said, 'Go get Dad.' I went to go get Dad, and he didn't realize what was happening. 'Dad, she's going home. I need you to come now.' We went back to the room, and there she was, in her own bed, in her jammies on her own pillow. My dad crawled into the bed next to her on one side, and I was on my knees by her side on the floor. She seemed to be struggling, and I put a washcloth on her forehead. She was holding my hand and my dad's hand. She let go of mine, and she brushed my father's hand from hers.

"That was the moment we knew she was going. Her face changed—it looked just like it used to when I was a little girl, and we were watching *The Little House on the Prairie* during an emotional scene, and she was about to cry from the joy of the happy ending—like she couldn't handle the overwhelming emotion. She had that same look on her face. I knew she had just seen Jesus.

"When she was diagnosed, she told me, 'What I want you to do, is I want you to get me to the finish line. And when I get to the finish line and see Jesus, let go of my hand and I'll walk across myself.' She had just let go of my hand, and she had that look on her face. I said, 'You made it. Go, Mom. Go. Run, you can run.' Nobody wanted her to fight, she had no reason to fight, and she said so herself. She had just had a final time of playing balloons with my kids, she had just pointed out the last thing she wanted to, she saw my husband and challenged him to a race. There was nothing left. She was ready. She didn't struggle. Her eyes were closed, and she was just gone. Everything was peaceful after that. There was no violent crying or weeping. My dad and I both were relieved. We felt blessed that she went so easy. My mom's entire life, she worried about when and how she was going to die. The minute she knew that was reality, that she was going to die, she was completely at peace."

JEN BABAKHAN

Love Has the Last Word

Shay Mason knew her father was drawing close to his heavenly home when he asked questions about his salvation soon after being baptized and coming to the Christian faith as a believer. "It was interesting to watch him as that transition began, as someone who had just become a Christian. They were giving him more medication to keep him comfortable, and you could tell that in his spirit he was reflecting on his whole life. He asked, 'Can I actually be forgiven for this?' as he talked about different things. He said, 'It's just too good to be true.' I told him that this was the one thing that isn't too good to be true. He asked us how he could know that he was really forgiven. My husband leaned over to him and said, 'I'm the priest that baptized you two weeks ago, you're forgiven—it's okay.' It was difficult to watch him deal with all of these things he had never dealt with before, but also beautiful too.

"The next day we brought our dog to be with him—he loved our dog more than anything on the planet. We put the dog in bed with him and I brought some pictures and just began showing him some photos. It made him really happy. Later that week, he began to be in and out of consciousness. On Friday, we began seeing the changes that happen at the end, and the hospice nurses said it could be at any time. It could be a few hours or more because his breathing was still stable. It was after eight o'clock that night, and we had to make the decision to leave the hospice center for the night or stay. We asked the nurse if she thought he would make it through the night and told her we would feel awful if it happened during the night and we weren't there. 'His breathing is still stable, so I would say go and get some rest. We'll call you if anything changes,' she said.

"We began packing our things to leave, and his breathing changed. 'Mom, I think this is it,' I said. She came over to him and held him and told him she loved him and began reminding him of some of their favorite vacations together. We held his hands and told him it was okay to go. He kind of coughed a little and took one big breath. With his last exhale, he said 'love.' That was it.

"I was shocked and turned to my husband. 'Did he say what I thought he said?' 'Yeah, he did,' he replied. I thought he may have been trying to tell us that he loved us, but I also think he entered into heaven. I felt the Lord had been saying to me all week, *His last breath on earth will be his first in heaven.* I prayed I would see transfiguration, and I think that's what I saw. I dreaded seeing him after he had died, but he looked amazingly peaceful and okay. I thought, if you told me a few years ago that I would ever do this—sit and hold somebody after they passed away—I would have said you were out of your mind. But it was beautiful, and it was right."

A Long Night

Being a critical care nurse, Mary Boswell is familiar with the dying process having witnessed it several times in her career. Still, watching her mother suffer in the weeks leading to her death proved to be a struggle. "As a critical care nurse, I had been in the room multiple times with dying patients, walking through those end-of-life moments. Each one is different. There were some very special and heartbreaking one-on-one moments with my patients when no other family was there. A week or so prior to her passing, my mom had a truly awful night. It was one of those nights where her pain and nausea were so bad, I sat on the bed holding her up while she was getting sick because she was so weak. I silently begged God to please either take her out of pain or take the pain away. I told him, *If you're not going to take this pain away from her, please just take her tonight.*

"As much as I didn't want her to go, I just begged Him to take her. He literally answered those prayers. From that night on, she had no more pain or nausea, which had been her biggest issue. The Lord answered that and, in His mercy, He gave her peace from that in the last week and a half of her life. When it was time for her to go, I got the call that her breathing had changed, and she was unresponsive. I knew then we were in the final hours. The death rattle is a natural part of the body releasing the soul. It's what our bodies go through, and there are times that my patients did pass away suddenly and quietly, but that isn't the norm. It's hard for the loved ones to accept, and it's difficult to listen to that cycle of breathing. I was there with my mom for fourteen hours as she passed away. I wanted to be there, and I wasn't going to be anywhere else."

When You Can't Be There

Not all of us can rush to our parent's bedside before they leave this world, and regardless of the reasons behind the absence, I believe we can only give ourselves grace. We do the best we can with the information available to us at that moment, with the relationships and resources we have at the time—and it's enough. God will bridge the gaps that we cannot fill, every time.

If you weren't able to be with your parent when they entered eternity, there is a tendency to hold on to guilt and regret because of your absence. While missing this moment feels like a loss in itself, I encourage you to remember it was just that—a moment.

The years that came before created the life of your loved one, and you were present for many, if not most of them. The unreachable standard that guilt tries to hold you to is not of God, nor of your parent.

While thoughts of regret may echo in your mind, I assure you, your parent is not spending a moment thinking of it now—and would prefer if you didn't either. Give yourself the gift of grace. If you're finding it hard to let go of deep feelings of regret and guilt, consider what you might tell your own child if they weren't able to be with you upon your passing, or what you might say to a friend in the same position.

Held by God Himself

Quantrilla Ard focused her energy into surviving the time of her mother's passing as everyone around her seemingly fell apart. "I really had to take the stance of, if I can just get through the first couple of weeks, I should be okay. I had this very stoic, flat effect, because I felt like I couldn't afford to fall apart because everyone around me was doing that. It wasn't the best way to cope through that, but it was my way. I didn't feel like I had time to cry and grieve. I had to get through it, survive it, and I thought

I would grieve and deal with it later. It is sort of the default way I handle hard times. I didn't have the capacity back then—it felt like everyone was looking at me to set the tone. They thought I was good.

"During this time of her becoming worse, I had the college class I was in, working to finish the coursework. I had a test coming up. I stayed overnight with her in the hospital one night because she wanted someone to be there. She told me to go home the next night to study in peace because she knew I had a final and the nurses would be coming in and out. I went home to study for the test and got a call from the hospital asking to speak to her husband. I got in touch with my father, and he went to the hospital. He called me inconsolable, saying they couldn't get her bleeding to stop, and she was sedated.

"We all rushed back to the hospital. I knew in my heart that this was it, and I was angry. I kept thinking, *This can't be happening right now, I thought I had more time,*. We arrived at the hospital, and she was intubated. I never got to speak to her again in a way that she could converse back with me. The nurses told us she was stable, and we should come back in the morning. I went home, but I knew I wouldn't see her again. I thought, *they said she's going to be okay*—but I didn't listen to my gut, and we went home. We got a call at 1:45 in the morning saying that her heart rate was dropping, and we needed to come back. We hurried back as fast as we could, but we missed it. We weren't there. To this day, if I could go back, I would. No one deserves to die alone. And even though it didn't feel like she was able to hear us or speak to us, I believe she could understand us. I wish I had just stayed. There's no comparison to this loss, even if you've known that the person has been sick for years, and you expect them to die, or if they're suddenly taken from you—there is no comparison. I can only hope that because she had such a strong relationship with God, that she could literally feel His arms surrounding and holding her so that she was not alone."

An Unexpected Sorrow

Sometimes a parent passes much sooner than you anticipate, under conditions you wish were different. For Becky Keife, her relationship with her father felt distanced at times, though they continued to get together for family events. "I saw him at Christmas. He wasn't doing especially well, but that was his normal. We were supposed to get together again in January, but I needed to reschedule it. He never called me back. He was always good about returning phone calls. I left a few messages and sent a couple texts, but I just had this gut feeling that he wasn't okay.

"I called my oldest sister to let her know I had been trying to get in touch with Dad. We decided that she would call his apartment complex and ask if he'd been seen recently. The apartment manager had a police officer come and do a wellness check. While I was waiting, I decided to take a walk with my baby and toddler—my daily sanity. I prayed with every step. As soon as I walked in the door, my phone rang. It was my sister. Dad was gone. They found him in his apartment. He had passed away from heart failure.

"I crumpled to the floor in tears. I sat there for a long time, holding both of my tiny sons, all of us crying together. I remember feeling so overwhelmed as a mom of young children. Loss and grief didn't stop diapers from needing to be changed, the baby needing to be nursed, or the laundry needing to be done. I didn't know how to process the pain while the demands of life marched on."

Birth and Death Within Eight Hours

Life is always a mix of joy and sorrow, but when two events, one elating and the other devastating, happen within the span of a day, emotions become even more complex. Becky McCoy was in labor with her first child, a boy, on the West Coast while her father lay in a hospital bed in his final hours in Connecticut. "We didn't know how much time my father had left, and it was three days before my due date. We decided to induce labor so I could try and get to the east coast as soon as possible. His nurses in Connecticut had my labor status up on his whiteboard next to his information and were coming in and checking with my parents whether I had the baby yet or not.

"I called my dad while I was laboring, to tell him we were naming our son after him—Caleb, because of the fierce determination my dad had. I didn't say goodbye as a final goodbye to him at the time, but I also knew it was the last time. I gave birth around eight o'clock Pacific Time, and my mom called at six thirty in the morning Eastern Time to let me know he had died. It was a lot to process at once. They showed him videos of Caleb before he died, but he had been on morphine for so long at that point. It was hard to know that one of the people I most wanted to meet my son was gone."

The Aftermath

Losing a parent is so surreal that the hours and days after can feel hazy and dream-like. After Mom died, I wondered, *Is this bottom? Is this the place I have been dreading for nearly three years?*

For a long time, I was filled with anxiety at the thought of her death, that when it finally occurred a sense of relief washed over me. Death was no longer an unknown experience, hovering like a rain-filled cloud above my every thought. It was a blissful sense of shock that surrounded me, permeated only by tears that sprang to my eyes without warning, a consistent release and processing my body clearly required.

The weeks that followed were a shock-tinged fog. The waves of grief ebbed and flowed, striking randomly through those first weeks, emotionally knocking me off my feet for a few minutes before allowing me to stand again. Everywhere I looked was a memory. Life felt blurry and out of focus while I moved through my days, doing normal activities—washing dishes or reading to my children. *She was just here. How is she not anymore? I can't call her.* I would think to myself, struggling to root myself in reality.

Death was no longer an unknown, but grieving my mother this way was new. This grief was different than the grief I felt when she was sick, and I knew death was coming. This grief had an emptiness to it that felt a bit terrifying. It felt bottomless, as if I stood on the edge of a great black hole, only a misstep from falling in.

During the day I could somewhat hold it at bay, blinking back tears while I made dinner, or placing my focus solely on my children and not the physical ache that now took residence in my chest. It was night that seemed to gently pull my mask away.

As the sun would set and the day's work had been done, the real work of grief waited for its turn. I knew that grief would have its way with me whether I fought it or surrendered. Instinctually, I knew it was better to wave the white flag from the start.

I remember my mother saying of her own grief, that she feared if she cried, her tears would never stop. I felt the same fear, and yet knew at some point there had to be a stopping point. I had read that the human body would not physically allow for a never-ending cry session—at some point, the tears dry up. I had to embrace what my soul was asking for if I wanted to move through the emotions in a healthy way.

And so I did. I allowed and embraced the heaving sobs each night as flashes of memories played like movies in my mind. I sobbed until I had no breath, until I was nauseated, and until I knew the grief was satisfied for that night. It wasn't a way to get over it, but it was a way to get *through* it, to the other side, where my heart was still broken, but the edges were wearing smooth like sea glass.

The Fear of Grief

After Mom died I remember wanting to "get the grief over with." I feared it in a very subtle way—I'm not sure I was conscious of just how much I feared what grief would do when it "really hit." It took a long while for me to see that my experience was just that—mine. Yours will be yours.

We love our parents uniquely and we will grieve them uniquely. In the years since, I've witnessed friends experience deep loss, and each time I recognize the desperation beneath their questions. *Am I grieving correctly? Am I crying enough? Will it feel this way forever?* The unspoken question is *Will I eventually be okay?*

You will be different in some ways, as you already know. But you will be okay. The grief will not swallow you. There is no correct way to grieve. Whether you cry all day or haven't shed a tear. Your way is your way. There is no reason to fear what grief will look like "when it hits," because friend, it is *already here*.

It may look different than what you expected, but it's *yours*. Let each moment lead you into the next with grace for what you do or don't feel. It's all welcomed. There is no "should" when it comes to grief. You can rest in that, and be where you are, even if this place is not the one you unexpected.

Sheer Exhaustion

Exhaustion arrives with deep grief that isn't often mentioned. I personally found that in the weeks and months after my mother's death, I needed to take naps during the day or go to bed earlier. When I slept, often after lying awake with tears streaming onto my pillow, it was a deep sleep, punctuated by vivid dreams, often of my mother.

Grief requires so much of the whole body—it has been one of the biggest proofs to me personally, that our bodies, souls, and mental state are indivisible. Grief calls for your rapt attention on every level a human being exists within. And the result is exhausting. It is vital you give yourself the space to be tired, amongst all the other things you are, in the days following the loss of your parent.

The Worst In Between

Each experience is unique and can differ wildly. Perhaps your grief shows itself as a quick temper, or an inability to find joy in what you used to. The stress of providing the best care, making appointments, and finding effective treatment is now the pressure of making funeral arrangements and planning to honor your parent best, while operating on autopilot through shock and grief.

For many of us, this time between death and the funeral feels like the worst in-between period of time that exists. I struggled with the knowledge that my mother's body was not in her home, and yet not in its final resting place either. It felt as though I could not feel peace myself until the funeral and her burial were complete.

She was already dancing in heaven, yet here on earth, I yearned for all of her to be at rest. Maybe you, too, have felt this way if your parent is already in heaven. I took comfort in knowing that our bodies are "tents" as the Apostle Paul would say, and that she truly was no longer here. If being away from the body is truly being home with the Lord (2 Cor. 5:8), we can take great comfort even in that space between death and burial. Our grief is still great and our sorrow still deep, but our mother or father is home with the Lord. We can rest knowing where they are, as we begin to find our own footing in this new world of ours without them.

Going Through Belongings

This topic is truly a personal decision, and one that may feel difficult or incredibly simple. For some, it feels easier to rid themselves of personal items such as clothing and toiletries right away, sort of like ripping off a bandage. For others, the idea of attempting to go through items so soon after the death is much too painful. Personally, I fell into the second camp. My brother and I decided on a middle ground with my mother's belongings. We would clear her items out of the main living spaces of the house to make it easier on my father.

In hindsight, I don't believe it mattered to have those items tucked away. Her absence was felt deeply whether her purse was in the chair she always set it in or not. The other things—medications and reminders of her last painful days—were a relief to get rid of. Our family had been in the fog of caregiving for so long, especially my father, that it was important to make his living spaces finally free of the reminders of so much pain and suffering. Those were reminders of the illness, however, not of *her*. Her items have been much more difficult to part with.

It's been more than three years, and we still have not donated her clothing. To be honest, I'm not sure we ever will. When I look at her clothing—the new tennis shoes she bought because "they were such a good deal" or the purse she saw at TJ Maxx and couldn't leave behind—the grief is still raw.

The smell of her perfume still wafts through the air and resides in her favorite pajamas, and for a moment, it seems impossible—unbelievable even. My mother is *gone*. I can barely see to type these words, the tears still fall fresh when I consider this truth, and this is why I don't have words of advice except to say: Do what feels right and brings you peace. Don't worry about what you *should* do. Do what you *want* to do.

Ultimately, decision fatigue made my decision for me. I couldn't decide if I would regret giving something away or not, so I just didn't. Eventually, I will. Perhaps I'll feel better after I do. For now, it gives me peace to know they are there. If you're struggling to get rid of items, you're not a hoarder. You're *grieving*. These things are in fact, just things. But they're what you have left of someone you deeply love. Be gentle with yourself.

A Moment for Mindfulness

For those struggling with memories related to witnessing their parent's death, or any post-traumatic stress related issues, Licensed Clinical Social Worker Sherry Lewis recommends seeking therapy with a trauma-informed therapist. "EMDR (Eye Movement Desensitization Reprocessing), a type of psychotherapy originally designed to alleviate the distress associated with traumatic memories, is very beneficial for all types of PTSD. People have different ways of processing emotional experiences, and this will determine, to an extent, what they find most helpful. For those with a bent toward auditory or verbal processing, they may find talking it out, or reliving the memory verbally to be a way of getting it out of their head and into the airspace. If you say it out loud and expose it, it returns the power back to you and releases any control the memory has over you. You don't want to ruminate on these memories, and the point is really to get them out of your head. If you're a visual processor, then writing the memory out can help. There is so much power in telling a story, and some people may find it helpful to write it and then read it."

If you weren't able to be with your parent at the time of death, Lewis says misplaced guilt can be an issue. "Guilt is an appropriate response when you've done something wrong. If you've missed a parent's death, whether it was in your control or not, you haven't done anything wrong. No law has been broken. More than likely, the feelings you're experiencing are sadness, regret, or disappointment. In our society it's more acceptable to feel guilt about something than sadness or grief. Grief makes people uncomfortable, because they don't always know how to handle it, but guilt they understand better."

Writing your parent a letter, and imagining their response can be a healthy way to process your feelings if you missed their death or any important moment. "You can write to them and say, 'I'm so sorry I missed your death, my heart was with you, even if I was not present.' If the parent was emotionally and mentally healthy, there would be no shame or guilt attached to their response to you. They would say something like, 'I know you love me and would have been there if you could, but we don't always have control over our circumstances or emotional ability to handle a difficult experience.' There can be peace found from a simple writing exercise like this one, to help someone sort out their misplaced emotions."

Consider:

- Which way would be most helpful to process the memories attached to your parent's death?
- What kind of processing works well for you in other difficult situations? Perhaps writing a letter to your parent after their death may be helpful in processing your emotions even if you were present for their passing.
- What would you say to your parent, and is imagining their response comforting to you?
- If your parent was not emotionally or mentally healthy, can you imagine what their response would be if they were?

A Daughter's Prayer

Father, only You know the depth of my grief. You have seen me in the quiet moments, the moments before sleep mercifully relieves my aching heart of its deep work to process this pain, unlike any I've felt before. I ask only that You sit with me in this dark place, a constant reminder of your faithful love and ever-present Light. Show me how to balance the grief I feel and the knowledge of the hope and eternal life my parent is now experiencing. Thank you for being a God who draws near to the broken hearted and binds our wounds. Help me know You are close. Amen.

NINE
WALKING THROUGH BROKEN GLASS
YOUR NEW LIFE, GRIEF, AND FAMILY ROLES

> There are no happy endings. Endings are the saddest part, so just give me a happy middle, and a very happy start.
>
> Shel Silverstein, *Every Thing On It*

The glow of the fire pit cast a warm glow upon my face while I held Carmela, Mom's beloved pup, inside my jacket under the starry night sky. She shivered against my chest that physically ached with grief. I looked up at the moon, wondering if somehow Mom was on the other side of it.

I knew she was in heaven with God, but the thing about heaven is that when someone you deeply love is there, you suddenly must know *where* exactly it is. Mom had died three days before.

Her death did not seem real. It felt as though she were home, sleeping like she had been so often lately, waiting for all of us to come visit. Zach invited us to his home for dinner that night. Our family had not been apart since the moment she left us. Bouncing back and forth between our two homes, we played games and watched movies, ate pizza, and laughed. Anything to keep us busy in the aching and ever-present void.

Mom was gone. And everything, in the span of a breath, the length of a single pulse, was now different.

No more running to the store for her favorite yogurt (the kind with very little sugar—anything else made her sick) or sparkling water (she never said no to the watermelon flavor). Medications still sat on the kitchen counter. A notepad with times she had last taken pills, written in my father's brisk handwriting sat beside them.

I wondered if their house—now my father's house—would ever feel the same. Mom was everywhere. The potholder hung from a cabinet door that I made her in sixth grade—my home economics teacher sewed it for me because even then I was not a domestic sewing goddess. A box of Kleenex and sponge-tipped mouth swabs sat next to the bed she died in, where all our lives were changed in ways none of us could accurately describe.

How were we to move on without her laugh punctuating our family gatherings and holidays? The void felt deep and dark enough to swallow me if I let it. And yet, I knew that for her we had to find our way through. We had to find a way of being a family again, with the heart that held us together missing.

One of the most unsettling times after the loss of your parent is the time between their last breath and your new normal as a family without them. The time is often marked by a sense of anxiety or unease as everything feels different—like a puzzle once satisfyingly complete now missing a piece in the very center.

Daily life feels different too. *Am I just supposed to go back to my life now?* The funeral was over. Condolences from others trickled to a stop. My mom was no longer a phone call away, or in her favorite chair at home with my father. She was *gone*.

The realization was both startling and familiar. Parts of me knew it as truth, and yet other parts didn't. Like when I would think, *Oh, Mom will laugh about this* or *I've got to call Mom later*, and then I would remember. When someone who has been in your life for every day of it is suddenly gone, it's as though every cell in your body must learn this truth slowly, and with a sort of resistance. It feels surreal. Wrong.

In the early days, I would wake in the middle of the night, and remind myself *Mom is dead*. I hoped that somehow if I reminded myself in the middle of the night, waking in the morning and remembering again wouldn't be so hard. Yet, each morning, right before my eyes fluttered open, I would need to remind myself again: *She's really gone.*

As the days wore on, the reminders became less and less necessary and I could sleep through the night again. I no longer needed the reminder. The truth had settled into me and became something I carried as much as my soul.

Mom was gone, and I was learning, somehow that she was still with me in some way. The mystery of it all still confounds me to this day. I hear her voice in my head when I need it most—always offering words of wisdom or even a joke about the situation at hand. She's both away and here, and none of it makes sense. But it doesn't have to. It simply is. And somehow, I still have a relationship with her. Her love is with me in every moment.

Perhaps this is the secret of dying and death—that for children of God, death doesn't *exist*. In the book of John, Jesus tells Martha after her brother, Lazarus, has died, "I am the resurrection and the life. He who believes in me will live, even though he dies; and whoever lives and believes in me will *never* die" (John 11:25-26, emphasis mine). A couple months after Mom died the truth of this verse settled upon my heart in a new and different way. I had seen her body die on that beautiful spring day—but *she* hadn't.

There wasn't a single moment that she was truly dead—not the true version of her. Her breath stopped here because where she was going, she had no need for it. She had no need for anything. The instant she left us, she was already in blissful paradise.

Jesus promised the thief on the cross next to Him that He would be in paradise *that day* with Him. There is no delay when it comes to the gift of eternity. There is a holy continuation of our lives—without a second of pause—even as we step into the promised paradise.

While you grieve your beloved parent, and make room for the absence that follows you into every space, make room for your new relationship with them too. Hearing their voice in your head doesn't mean you're in need of therapy—though it can be helpful. Not everything has or needs an explanation. Your new relationship with your parent can be as it is, if it brings you peace.

Letting Others In

While you may be tempted to withhold your grief from others because of the belief, "If they haven't been through it, they won't get it," that's also an isolating way to experience such a profound loss. The illness and death of a parent is a life-changing kind of grief. However, everyone understands what it is to grieve *something*.

In the depths of my grief, when it felt unbearably heavy, I would send out a simple text to my closest friends: *I'm really sad about my mom right now, can you pray for me?* It felt like a very vulnerable thing to say, and yet their responses only validated that I *should* be really sad, my mother had died, and they were honored to pray. I always felt the heaviness lift from my shoulders and heart when I told them in plain, simple language: *I feel sad. Please pray.*

Becky McCoy also felt a need to acknowledge her emotions about her father's death in a different way. "I learned so much from his death. I learned to acknowledge what I was feeling. I had the real 'good girl' ability to pretend that I didn't have emotions, or they didn't affect me. I had to really wrestle with that, and learn to say, 'I'm sad today. I wish Dad was here' instead of 'It would be cool if Dad was here, but he's not, so I'll talk myself right out of these emotions.' It was a huge thing for me to realize how disconnected from my emotions I was. Grief felt unproductive to me. I thought if I could outthink the grief, if I could think through it, then I could process it and move past it. Grief is a process and the only way to work through it is to work through it. It took me until about year two to start grieving. I was dealing with my own unhealthy ideas and habits toward emotional grief even though I had been through it so many times already. I had been joking that funerals were my hobby."

It's important we don't leave our spouses out of the loop either. Ed had lost his father three years before Mom died, and I admittedly was oblivious to just how life-changing the loss of a parent could be at the time. I was blessed to have a partner who understood the agony and anguish of it all, even though I felt like no one could truly understand my pain because my relationship with my mother was my own and no one else's.

That's true for you, too, even if you have siblings. Each familial relationship is unique in itself. When a death occurs, that fact feels both comforting and isolating. Regardless of whether your spouse has experienced the loss you have, I believe it is a positive thing to share your experience with them.

Mary Boswell remembers this time in her life well. "I remember having days when I would just text my husband and say, 'Today's a hard grief day. I don't know how to do what I've got to do today. I don't know if I can even get up off the couch today.' He would respond, 'It's okay. You do what you have to do. It's going to take time.' And it did take time. I thought because we had walked through it with his parents, I had been there, done that—I've got this. It was different though because it was my mom. I thought it was the same but it's not the same. I had many days where I just kind of sat, and getting the laundry done and folded was an accomplishment."

Complicated Grief

I would be remiss in writing about post-death grief if I didn't mention the nature of complicated grief that results from a complex or difficult relationship with a parent. I don't know that anyone has a purely blissful adult relationship with his or her parent one hundred percent of the time. I think each of us can see ourselves a bit in the complicated grief experience. Perhaps we didn't always apologize for hurts caused or strained words spoken. It's possible that we were still waiting for apologies that never came from a parent. Or maybe we didn't visit enough, or our parent had a mental disorder or illness that made time spent together tense.

It is possible to grieve someone while acknowledging that our time together was not always good. Often, if your relationship was a difficult one, you may feel undeserving of the feelings of grief you're now experiencing. You may wonder *If I didn't feel this depth of love for them while they were here, how can I feel this devastated about their death?*

The answer is, you are entitled to feel *however* you feel. There is a tendency to idolize and glamorize someone after their death. We've all heard the saying, "Don't speak ill of the dead." However, this doesn't mean we lie to ourselves. The relationship you had, and on some level still have, with your parent is yours and yours alone.

Life is difficult and complex. People can be as well. You can wish things were different *and* feel as though you love them more than you ever have, even in life. I think part of the both/and-ness of it all is that we can now sense that our parent is healed and whole in heaven—free of every aspect that made life here difficult or less than what we hoped. Free of the things that held them back. They can now just love us, from a place of purity they've never been able to access before, in the very presence of God.

There is a very real sense of grief you may feel in knowing the relationship you dreamed of having with your parent is no longer an option. Allow yourself to feel it and know this is a loss on its own—it's the death of a dream your heart has held onto for a long time. It's okay to take the time to process and mourn it.

For Becky Keife, whose relationship with her father was complex, grief brought up some unexpected emotions. "Throughout the stages of grief, one thing I didn't expect to feel was guilty. Part of that guilt came from missing my dad. Because our relationship was complicated, there were times I dreaded getting together. Now that he was gone, I felt like, 'What right do I have to miss him in death? I didn't miss him in life.' I also felt guilty over a small sense of relief. With my dad, there was always a feeling of 'What's going to happen next? When are we going to have to drop our lives again and show up for him?' This was a reflection of a rollercoaster cycle of up-and-down crisis in my dad's life. So there was guilt because it was easier with him gone. I had to grapple with the fact that that's true and yet also heartbreaking.

"There is also the part that is grieving the dad I lost and grieving the dad that I needed and never had. I struggled to know what this looked like because my grief wasn't the same as the person who lost their father who was also their best friend. Eventually I had to accept that my grief, my missing, and my longing for my father were still valid. I realized I can celebrate what was good without dismissing the hard. And I can also acknowledge what was bad without erasing the good. I learned to hold both at the same time."

JEN BABAKHAN

A Word About Therapy

A highly sensitive person, I have to shield myself from media and news that's too traumatic or violent in nature. Those kinds of images have a way of getting stuck in my mind. I try to protect my sensitive mind like I protect my children from seeing things I know they shouldn't. I knew on some level that witnessing my mother's death would be traumatic, even if it wasn't violent—the emotional experience of my brain and heart comprehending the event alone would be enough to trigger and affect my inner child.

I knew I needed help processing the event in some way, though I wasn't sure how to go about it. I did know that something in me was *certain* I needed to write it out, but that felt too risky. What if, when I wrote the event out, in painstaking detail, it triggered tears that never stopped? That sounds irrational now, but my grief-brain thought it made perfect sense. I put the thought of writing it down out of my mind and decided to handle it in a different way—by not doing anything.

A few months after Mom died, a beloved uncle was diagnosed with cancer. It all came rushing back in an instant—memories of scans and hospitals, appointments, and statistics. Images of my mother after her death would not leave my mind. Flashes of her body haunted me at random moments during the day while I cooked dinner or read a book. Suddenly, I was right next to her bed again, watching her pulse slow to a stop. I would blink back tears and will myself to come back to the present moment.

During the COVID-19 pandemic, I contacted an online therapist and gave her the quick rundown of the last three years of my life. I ended with my newly diagnosed uncle, and the disturbing intrusive thoughts and images that would not stop playing like a movie reel in my mind.

"I feel like I should write it all down," I said, "everything that happened when she died."

"Why don't you?" she asked.

"Because I might cry and never stop."

"I'd like you to try it—just try—before our next meeting," she said.

And I did. I tucked myself into our bedroom and wrote, in excruciating detail, every moment of my mother's dying experience. The words, not organized in anything but a stream of consciousness, poured out of my heart. Tears fell onto the pages. I wrote until my hand hurt. When I was done, I released a long, cleansing sigh. It was *out of me*.

At the next session I told the therapist that I completed the homework. Surprising to no one but me, the intrusive images were gone.

"You got them out and onto the page," she said. "They exist somewhere else now. They don't have to live in your mind constantly."

Grief therapy wasn't a huge breakthrough or even something I continued for any length of time, but it was a place to cry and feel validated. A place to hear "Of course you're sad and tired and triggered. *Of course* you are." It was a scheduled appointment to stare into my heart and acknowledge its broken pieces. It was a place to tell someone else about my mom, her sense of humor, and how very much I missed her deep in my bones. Therapy for me was confirmation of what I already knew—that I needed to write my pain down. I just needed the push to do it.

If you have access to therapy, I encourage you to try it at any point in time. If your parent utilized hospice services, the hospice company will often provide free grief counseling for the first year after the death. Support groups exist as well for adult and child grievers either online or in person, typically at hospitals, cancer treatment centers, and local churches. I encourage you to seek out opportunities to share your grief with someone else, however that may look, that are available to you in your area.

A Word on Suicidal Thoughts

This goes without saying, but I would be irresponsible if I did not mention it: If you are having suicidal thoughts, feeling suicidal, or feel that your grief is overwhelming you to the point of making a plan to end your life—PLEASE DON'T. This is your sign not to. Help is available right this moment. You can reach the National Suicide and Crisis Prevention Lifeline, by dialing 988.

New Grief Revives Old

It makes sense to me now, but at the time I was shocked by how visceral my reaction was to my uncle's cancer diagnosis. I wanted to be as helpful as I could while managing my own triggered emotions and traumatic response.

A while later, when our eighteen-year-old cat died, I again found myself dealing with old grief rising again to the surface. It felt as though the loss of my mother magnified every new grief into something much larger than it would have been before.

When grief becomes compounded in this way, it's easy to get lost in which emotion is tied to which circumstance. It all begins to feel like one giant ball of sadness, its origin indistinguishable. Even if you aren't sure where the emotion comes from, and it feels like a disproportionate response to the event that triggered you, I encourage you to go with it. Let the grief, silly or overdramatic as it may seem, sit with you instead of shaming yourself for its presence.

I have found that my responses to awful things in the news or things that happen to friends of friends affect me greatly. Sometimes I grieve that nothing about this world feels right, and I yearn for the perfection that must exist in heaven. Grief, however it comes to you, comes to bring healing. Let it. Welcome it. Your body, mind, and soul will thank you.

Seasonal Shifts

Just as I experienced emotional changes approaching holidays, I noticed I also experienced something similar as the seasons changed—particularly the springtime, as this was both the season of her diagnosis and death. It was almost as though the sights and smells of sunny days and blooming flowers were a portal back in time, to crying in hospital corridors and standing beside a heart-shaped flower arrangement beside the freshly dug grave. Even still, a beautiful day with fluffy clouds reminds me of the day we watched her leave us. I am continually amazed how our senses record details we aren't aware of until we find ourselves reacquainted with them at another time.

You might find it helpful to be aware of how the seasonal shifts may affect you when the anniversary approaches of your parent's diagnosis or death anniversary. Awareness is key and allows you to be gentle with yourself in meaningful and effective ways. When the weather turns springlike and I feel the familiar fatigue creep into my body, I give myself grace. I'll think something along the lines of *Yes, this is the time everything changed, and you were in a deep sense of grief. It makes sense you are more tired. It makes sense that everything feels a little tender these days.*

If you are aware of the timing of it all, you are able to try and rid yourself of negative self-talk related to your energy level, or lack thereof, and anything else you might be tempted to shame yourself about. This is the time of year to hold yourself extra close and give yourself what you need most.

New Family Roles

Navigating how to care for your remaining parent in their new life, while also maintaining your own family needs, can be difficult to manage simultaneously.

My mother wrote each of us a letter after she was diagnosed, giving us words of advice and her hopes for us after she was gone. In mine, she wrote that I was now the caretaker of the family. It wasn't a role I ever wanted, but it was one I was honored to step into.

As time has passed, I've learned there is no real family caretaker in her absence, but we each take care of one another in our own way. In the beginning, I struggled to know how to make our family gatherings feel full enough to make up for her absence. The truth was, and still is, I cannot.

A loss this great in a family is always present, and there is no use trying to cover it up, or fill the void your parent left. I learned it's best to just let it be. Let there be silence where their laughter once filled the room. Let there be an empty chair at the table. Let yourself speak of what he or she would have done, or said, or liked. It's in the spaces of silence and tear-filled eyes that we remember and honor our loss and our love that will co-exist until we are with them again.

Making Adjustments

Before my mother died, I spoke to her almost daily on the phone, usually around four in the afternoon. Sometimes the afternoon is when I miss her the most, because I long to hear her voice while I prepare to make dinner or ask my boys to stop arguing for the thousandth time.

My father and I have always had a close relationship but chats on the phone weren't a regular part of it. Finding a new way of being a daughter to my father without my mom involved was another new normal to adjust to. Surprisingly, Dad loves to talk on the phone, or he pretends to for my sake, and we talk on the phone several times a week, usually in the evening.

We also visit one another at least once a week, which is thankfully easy because of our close proximity. I enjoy going to his house and having long chats together while our dogs play in the backyard or inviting him over for dinner and video games with my boys. Sometimes, I allow myself to zoom out a bit and think of the big picture of how far our family has come, and I can feel my mom's pride in how we've carried on without her.

Trying to Make it Better for the Surviving Parent

One thing that seems common in my observance of others who have lost parents, is the desire to somehow lessen the grief of the surviving parent. It may be a struggle to decide how much to include them in your activities, even if they weren't typically a part of family vacations or certain celebrations.

If this is a struggle for you, I think it's incredibly important to determine where your motivation stems from. Is it a simple desire to include the living parent in your life more now that you know what it's like to lose one? Or is it coming from a place of wanting to reduce your surviving parent's time and ability to grieve?

I believe the first is a worthy endeavor and the latter a mistake. While no one wants a parent to suffer, and certainly not alone, it is a natural and necessary part of grieving a spouse to have time and space to do so in solitude. We cannot spare them this pain, though we wish desperately we could.

I believe including your remaining parent in your family's activities is incredibly healthy and important for everyone involved, if it comes from the right place. My boys have needed their grandfather to be present and active in their lives in the way he always has been, but I knew early on that I couldn't take my father's pain away. It wasn't my responsibility to do so.

Our parents are on their own paths in this life and grief is a part of it. Not to be swept to the side, or ignored, but experienced. As their adult children, we can support them in the ways they also support us. We reminisce, we laugh, and we miss them, together.

Sophie Hudson experienced a slight change in her relationship with her father that was unexpected but sweet. "There has been a gradual and real tenderness that I feel like we have seen in him. He's more vulnerable with us and shares a lot more. I feel like he's felt more comfortable giving us all the sides of his life—he was a parent our whole life, and he still is our parent, but I feel like when Mama was diagnosed, he really became more of a friend. He never called me before. When I got married, it was always Mama who called. He calls me now. I wrote about when Mama died in my last book, and when Daddy read it, he sent me the sweetest email. He said it wasn't until he read that book that he felt like he really grieved her. He was able to sit with it. I feel like I know him more fully as a person now than I ever have."

Including Your Children

While you may be working to create a new normal with your parent, keep in mind that your children can be vital in the process. Often this is overlooked as we tend to take plans and situations onto our own shoulders, rather than include our children, who know and love their remaining grandparent.

For Jaime Jo Wright, this meant her daughter making her grandmother's favorite recipes and taking them to her grandfather. "There have been a lot of different family dynamics, and my father has early Alzheimer's disease which brings up a whole other dynamic. We've gotten closer thorough it. My daughter feels like she promised Nanny that she would take care of Poppy. She makes sure that she gets over to his house to bake him his cookies and muffins that my mom always baked. She's been doing that for two years, and he's hardly gone without her cookies and muffins. It's her same recipe and he lives off those. There's an element of responsibility that the kids have taken on, and it's been good for them. My dad has said many times, how he has friends who've lost wives and they're now on their own without interaction with their family. We are over there with him twice a week."

Accepting Unexpected Family Changes

Not all shifts in families are positive after a death. With emotions running high and a lack of normal rhythm, things can change quickly, and not always for the better. Relationships, if not handled carefully and with a lot of communication, can suffer as a result.

Before her mother passed, Quantrilla Ard promised she would make a life for herself away from home. "I didn't anticipate the lack of continuity in some of my family relationships. A lot of my family relationships changed, and not necessarily in a horrible way, but in a way I just wasn't prepared for. It was rough. My mom was the gatherer, she was the central person everyone gathered around, but she told me I needed to go once she was gone. She told me I needed to move on and live my life, whatever that looked like. And so I did."

For Becky McCoy, her experience with family after the loss of her father was layered. "It was hard because my mom and sister had been together with my dad when he died, so they had a lot of processing and grieving that experience. Because I wasn't there, I couldn't share that with them. It was extra isolating because their grief was very different from mine. They were also dealing with the trauma of having been with Dad. Not only was I not with them when he died, but I also couldn't be with them through that part of their grief. It was hard to know whom I could grieve with. I had my own kind of trauma, but it wasn't that. I was there with a newborn trying to figure out where I fit in now, because I didn't have this shared experience, and it was really hard."

"My mom and I actually went to therapy together because there were a lot of things happening that were codependent behaviors from both of us. If we didn't nip it in the bud they were going to be the end of our relationship. After my dad died, my sister, mom, and I would travel or go out to lunch together to try to connect. When my sister moved home after grad school to be with my mom, and I had moved home to Connecticut after my husband died, we were all in the same town. It really helped us to re-establish our relationships with each other as adults, and to set a new baseline of who our family was now. There was a lot of intention behind it, you can't just hope everyone figures it out. You have to be intentional about what you're missing and what doesn't feel good, or what you need, and what you can offer."

Families are forever changing, even in good times. They expand and shrink, much like the impact that grieving has on our lives. Like many other things in life, acknowledging the truth, regardless of what it may be, goes a long way in healing what is asking to be healed within yourself and your family.

If you're not sure of the way forward, ask God for direction. He holds it all—the complicated grief, your confusion about shifting family dynamics, and the emotions you would rather not face head on—within His grasp.

A Moment for Mindfulness

Family dynamics can get tricky after a death, according to Clinical Psychologist Barbara Greenberg, PhD. "I've seen families become more cohesive after a death and some that became more fractured, because it was the parent that held the family together. The siblings that are with a dying parent together, who each took a role and were able to be vulnerable together—those are the ones that typically have or create a deep connection with one another. When someone's dying, you kind of have to be there—it's not a time where you can make an appointment to see one another later. You're forced to sit together and share in this experience. It's such a big deal when people show up for you in times of need, it can save your life."

Consider:

- How would you say your family handled the news of your parent's terminal diagnosis? If your parent has passed, how have they handled the death? In what ways do you wish it was different, and in what ways was it beneficial? If there is more you would change about the experience than keep the same, it isn't too late to work on building those relationships after the fact. A good first step is being open to speaking about the experience, and how you foresee yourselves as a family moving forward.

A Daughter's Prayer

Lord, You are the same when nothing else in my life is. You know how different it feels now, how unsettled I am, and how much I long for a new sense of normal. Please heal relationships in my family where healing is needed. Show me what is broken and needs mending and give me Your guidance at each step of the way. Father, give me courage to be vulnerable with others and myself. Help me to let others know when I need them to pray on my behalf. Give me the strength to process this pain in a healthy way that honors You and my parent. Thank you, Father, for Your nearness in this sorrow. Amen.

TEN
RESILIENT HOPE
EMBRACING THE FINALITY OF DEATH WITH PEACE

In my deepest wound I saw your glory, and it astounded me.
Saint Augustine

I watched Ed and the boys play flag football with the rest of our little family—my brother Zach and his wife, Berenice, and my father. They laughed and tossed the ball back and forth, taking dives to snatch one another's blue or yellow flag from their belt.

It was a cool October day, and the gentle breeze through the park felt soft and welcoming. An empty lawn chair sat to my right. *Mom would have sat next to me and we would have loved watching this together*, I thought. Our family was different now without her. I was different now. The months without her passed quickly, permeated by moments of piercing grief, when the reality of life without her came rushing back without permission.

Grief Through the Years

"The thing is," I texted Zach one afternoon when sharing about how much I missed our mother, "she just keeps being ... dead." And that is the struggle for those of us left here on this side of heaven. Death feels final, and the void our parents leave feels gaping.

The first year without my mother felt hazy. Everything we did together without her was like listening to a piano slightly out of tune. I heard from others repeatedly that the second year after a death is harder than the first. *How can that be?* I thought.

And then the second year arrived, and I understood. Their absence seems to settle in a bit more at the two-year mark. During this year it began to feel like a very long time since I last heard her voice, or felt her arms surround me in a hug. I forced myself to listen to her voicemails I saved, as much to get it over with as anything else. It just felt like something I needed to do. As soon as I heard my mother's voice I crumbled. A voice as close to my heart as its own beat, and I had not heard it in so long.

When I watched videos I saved of her on my phone, sitting next to my boys or making conversation with my father, it felt surreal. *I know her every move, her every mannerism, like the back of my hand. And she's gone. How is she gone?* The depth of my grief felt bottomless. *This is what it is now and will continue to be.* I was wrong.

The third year felt softer in every way, as though my grief no longer required tear-filled moments, but only a gentle acknowledgement of its presence. *There you are*, it seemed to want me to whisper. *I see you.*

In my fourth year without my mother, I've learned that grief does not lessen over time, but it does become easier to live with. It still shows up unexpectedly—like a party guest you made a point not to invite. Grief no longer barges in and rearranges your plans. Now, it sits in a corner and taps its foot until you give it the attention it requests.

Learning to live again, side by side with a grief that sometimes reappears without warning, is a new way of living entirely. Things that never used to trigger emotion suddenly stop me in my tracks. Our children, too, are now living different lives, in this *after* place of loss. How do we help them process this new experience, when we are new ourselves to this landscape?

A year after Mom died one of my boys said, "It will never be the same without Grandma."

I replied with the only words that came to me: "You're right. It won't ever be the same, but it can still be good."

Now that grief and I are very good friends, I trust it more and more. I know it will appear when I need it to—even if I'm certain I don't need it at all. I now trust that it serves me in ways I cannot fathom. I trust grief to do its job within me. And I trust that every time I fall apart, I will come back together.

As this trust has been built with grief, I no longer fear its arrival. I no longer experience the same anxious thoughts that once bounced through my mind. *What if I start sobbing when we open Christmas presents? What if grief ruins Mother's Day? What if I make everyone feel weird with my crying?* I trust grief to be present, honest, and helpful, all at the same time—like a good friend should be.

Riding the Waves

It has been my experience that peace is possible in the loss of our parent when we accept all that loss brings, as well as all it has taken. Our lives are forever different now, but we can own the differences and be proud of how they have grown our lives and our faith.

Sophie Hudson finds the unexpected times of grief remind her that loss will forever be with her, as much as her love for her mother will be. "I have learned it comes in waves, that it hits in unexpected times. There are times it pops up, where you don't see it coming, but you think, *God, I really miss my Mama.* This particular death has been the deepest grief I have personally experienced. Sometimes I'm surprised when it shows up and I'll think, *Oh, it's still here.* I thought grief was gone, but it's still here and I think it always will be. That was a deep, long, and pivotal relationship in my life. It's kind of like a neighbor who you don't see very often, but every once in a while it just kind of pops to the surface. It's not that it doesn't hurt as much. That part doesn't change. You miss your mama, and there are times you just want your mama. The ache is specific, and I think it will be with me forever. I've also learned that grieving is better when it's done openly and with people who loved the same person you do."

Becky Keife also describes the grief during the first years without her father as being like a wave. "It's been a little more than twelve years since my father passed, and the emotions now are less intense. In the first two years there would be times it felt like grief was a tidal wave I didn't see coming—I'd be in the grocery store and break down with no clue what hit me. The ocean—the ebb and flow of the waves—is such good picture of grief. It's not linear, you don't go through clean and clear stages and then you're over it. There's never an 'over it.' I find though that, overall, the swells are gentler. I don't feel overcome by grief in the ways I used to.

"I've learned a lot of tools over the years and how to make space for my grief. For example, my dad loved baseball, and I often feel that swell of grief as I watch my three sons play and think of how my dad would have loved to be there watching them too. Now, I've learned not to judge that grief in myself, but to let it rise, wipe the tears, and move through it. Early on, I tried harder to push it down. But just like when someone is being pummeled by a wave, if they try to fight against it, it only gets that much harder. It's better to relax your body into it. This doesn't mean you still won't get rocked, but you will pop out of that tumultuous wave sooner than if you were fighting and struggling against it."

Doing Something

For some, taking action in some way to honor your parent can help you feel more at peace. This outward expression of love toward a project of some sort creates a place for the unexpressed emotions to flow in a constructive way. Personally, I found visiting the cemetery after my mother's death to be too difficult and jarring. *Is there something wrong with me? Is this denial?* I wondered each time I drove away from her grave feeling regretful about my visit. "She's not there, not really," I told my dad after a visit. "It feels weird to visit her body when I feel more connected to her just in nature or anywhere else, really."

For some, visiting the grave and making sure it looks nice is an act of love that feels productive and right. For others, it doesn't. Both are okay. Your grief experience is just that—*your* grief experience.

On my mother's first birthday after her death, I planted a rose bush in our backyard in her honor. *This is how Mom would want me to remember her*, I thought as Ed and the boys worked to dig the hole together to plant the rose. My boys were excited to plant something "for Grandma."

Each spring it blooms with the most vibrant cream and pink colored blossoms I have ever seen. The first spring twelve blooms arrived at once and I felt as though Mom sent me a dozen roses. Extravagant and beautiful, the rose bush now sits as a reminder of my mother's life, and her love for each of us.

Nearly four years after Mom died, I hosted a baby shower for Zach and Berenice. This will be the first grandchild, a boy, whom my mother won't meet on this side of heaven. The day felt joyful and bittersweet—a mix we've become all too familiar with. Earlier that morning, I noticed a bloom at the front of the rose bush. It was stunning, with hot pink lining the edges of each petal and a soft yellow cream center that reminded me so much of my mother. I knew she had something to do with this beauty blooming on this special day.

Midway through the shower, my aunt noticed the gorgeous bloom. "It has two centers!"

I had taken a photo of it earlier and somehow missed the incredible fact that the flower had two centers, twisted tightly next to one another. It felt like a gift, straight from heaven. Mom not only knew about her grandson, she let us know she sent her love on that day.

For Jaime Jo Wright, a barn cat reminded her that God and her mother's love were still watching over her. "For the first year and a half my dad kept saying he didn't want an animal. He's always loved our twelve-year-old barn cat, Maddie, whom my mother named. I decided on my way to my dad's one day to take her with me. She'd never been in the car or even left our farm.

"I took her to my dad's house and opened the door, and right away she ran in, lay on the floor, and started purring. This is a cat that should be terrified, like most cats would be. She followed him around like a dog. When I went to go home, Dad said, 'You're not taking her home are you?' I told him I was planning on it, but it didn't look like she wanted to go. 'Go get litter and food. She's here and she's home,' he said and started crying. She's brought him so much joy—it's totally a God thing, she's never been an inside cat."

Sometimes, a public remembrance feels right. Becky McCoy's father was the Director of Public Works in their town. What began as a simple gesture, became something much bigger over the years. "They had named the Public Works Building after him. Around year three we began bringing donuts for all the guys at the Public Works Building on my dad's birthday. The town still does a blood drive in honor of Dad's birthday. And after the first year we began a golf tournament to raise money for clean water projects in Haiti. My dad was a civil engineer, and his dream was to finish his career and do clean water projects all over the world. It was a way for us to honor his dream. There's a boardwalk in town along the water that was destroyed during Hurricane Sandy.

"The boardwalk was Dad's pet project. He wanted to turn downtown into a place people wanted to come visit and go to restaurants, and it is now. He wanted lampposts up and down Main Street, and now each Christmas there is a Main Street Stroll for small business shopping. Seeing the wreaths lit up around the lampposts is like seeing his handprint on everything. To raise funds to rebuild the boardwalk, they sold benches, and we bought him a bench.

"It's right near an ice cream parlor, which is a huge thing in my family. We're kind of known for our love of ice cream. Now we go get ice cream and walk to Dad's bench. My sister got engaged at the bench. We've found ways to include him as life continues, and I think that's what my family needed more than calendar-based traditions."

Becky Keife says, "My dad loved pie. It's one of the things we shared. If he came to my high school basketball game or musical, he would ask me if I wanted to go out for pie afterwards. On my father's birthday this past year, I bought a pie. It was a simple but meaningful way to celebrate and honoring my dad."

The smallest of gestures can bring great happiness to our hearts. If we listen, our hearts ask us for the simple recognition that remembering matters.

A Word About Health Anxiety

A common theme amongst those who have lost a parent, especially to terminal illness, is experiencing health anxiety, which is a fear of contracting a serious or life-threatening illness. It can cause a hyper-focus on certain sensations or feelings, leading to a false correlation with a serious condition. For some, this looks like panicking when their heart skips a beat or repeatedly checking their blood pressure to make sure it's within the proper range. For others, it may include taking their temperature or researching symptoms of a certain illness. It may or may not be the same illness their parent died of.

Left unchecked, health anxiety can easily take over a person's life, and it's important to seek help from a professional if you feel this is what you're experiencing.

It makes logical sense that watching a parent be diagnosed, treated or not, and experience death from an illness would trigger within us an innate desire to protect ourselves from the same fate. This natural goal of keeping ourselves safe can trick us into a sort of hyper-vigilance that becomes the filter through which all sensations or pains are filtered.

In my own experience, health anxiety is sneaky, and shows itself during times when I'm feeling more stressed or tired than usual. Just like grief, each of us will have a different response to the stress our bodies feel as a result of loss. It's important to keep tabs on any feelings of doom regarding your health, or a sense that it is inevitable you will follow on your parent's path. I recommend seeking the advice of a qualified mental health professional to help you remain logical and rational when your anxious brain tries to steer you in the opposite direction.

Also, if your parent died young, health anxiety or a feeling of general fear may arise when you reach or approach the age your parent at the time of their death. Even subconsciously, you may have assumed that you, too, will die early or around the same age. It is important to stay aware of the stories we tell ourselves, consciously or not, about our health and our future. Again, therapy is a valid option for working out these beliefs in a helpful setting rather than sitting at home and ruminating about them.

Living Again with Enthusiasm

One of the things about death is that if we let it, death can teach us how to live. We become aware that life on earth is indeed short and finite.

It pushes us to reconsider our lives and the choices we make about how we spend our time. If this is it—our one and only life here—what will we do to honor this gift of time? What do *we* want to be remembered for? If we lived like heaven was real, every day, what would our living look like?

One of the most intriguing parts of witnessing my mother's journey through cancer and her knowledge of her own mortality was the sense of peace she had when nothing more could be done. Even when she was freshly diagnosed, she asked that we pray for God's will to be done. There was no panic or anger, just peace and contentment with the life she had.

At one point, she told me she felt cancer had been a gift, as it had given her perspective on life, and drawn her closer to God. In a way, cancer and living the rest of her life with determination had given her a true sense of purpose.

Those of us who have witnessed the brevity of life and the finality of death know in a different way than others what it means to live and die. It's why we feel as though others who have gone through it are in a sense, part of the same club that none of us wanted to join. Yet here we are, with this first-hand knowledge of a widely known fact: This life is meant to be lived, truly lived, in service of one another and God.

Knowing death in this intimate way has changed our lives and perspective. After my mother's death, I was struck by the cyclical nature of life, and how closely death mirrored birth. Certainly, there is much to be gained by using this new knowledge of ours in both big and small ways. It's more than making a "bucket list." It's living each day with the intention of using the time to connect deeply to both our lives on earth and our soul connection with our Creator.

My aunt gave my son her old guitar. We put him into lessons, and he learned the basics. As I watched him learn, I thought about my own childhood dream of learning to play an instrument. My parents weren't financially able to put me into lessons or afford an instrument rental. By the time I got into the upper grades the dream faded and it felt as though it were too late to pursue as a beginner. *Why couldn't I learn now? What if I taught myself to read music, at the very least?*

And so I did. I taught myself to read music and purchased a digital piano, one that wouldn't take up too much space in our home. I practiced simple piano lessons daily while watching YouTube tutorials. Learning to play, ever so slowly—painfully so—has taught me that small joys can connect us to something bigger than ourselves.

There was something spiritually shifting within myself, with each chord progression, with each new song. It was as though a light switched on in a dark room of my soul—one that had never been lit before but had been waiting all along. My dream of creating music had never truly died, it only waited for the right time to be born into my life. I'm not a natural pianist—far from it. I plank out notes with my much-too-short-to-play-more-than-a-fifth-note fingers, and I feel my soul smile from within. *You're doing it,* I tell myself. I can feel my mother smiling when I sit down at the bench to work out this thing that is only for joy. Things that are done solely for joy are worthy of our time.

Jesus modeled this for us when he changed water into wine at the wedding at Cana. Though He was hesitant to perform this miracle as His first. He told Mary His time had not yet come when she told Him the bride and groom had run out of wine. So, He saved them of humiliation and provided them with what they needed to impress the master of the banquet and keep the party going. Jesus knows that our small joys matter to us, and I believe He delights when we find them again—or for the first time—after a period of sorrow and grief.

One of the best ways to rediscover a love of life again is to be open to the ways God may be drawing you closer, even if they feel slightly unconventional. I've found He uses all sorts of circumstances and people to place us on the path He's set for us in this time of our lives.

A friend gifted me a Yoga for Grief online course three years after Mom died, and though I was hesitant to try yoga specifically for grief I decided to give it a chance. After the first session I was convinced I had found a new way to connect to my body's experience of grief and help it process it through a time of movement and connection to God. It was unlike anything I had ever experienced. It was a gift I didn't know I desperately needed and set me on a path of uncovering a more intimate connection with the parts of my grief story still calling for my attention. I continue to practice yoga nearly daily, simply because of the connection to God I feel during each session.

A Life Surrendered to Love

Perhaps the most surprising fact of losing a parent to a terminal illness is that we survived the ordeal. It may feel as though we barely did, but here we are. Here you are. Despite our deepest wishes and even prayers, we have grown wiser through this pain. We have learned things we wish we never had to, and we trust God to bring something of value through us and into this world, full of broken and grieving souls.

Deep grief has given us new and profound empathy for others we can now use to share the love of Christ. Paul writes in the 2 Corinthians, "Praise be to the God and Father of our Lord Jesus Christ, the Father of compassion and the God of all comfort, who comforts us in all our troubles, so that we can comfort those in any trouble with the comfort we ourselves have received from God. For just as the sufferings of Christ flow over into our lives, so also through Christ our comfort overflows" (2 Cor. 1:3-5).

We have experienced the deep comfort of the God of all comfort, so how can we now let it flow through us into others? Before my mother was diagnosed with cancer, I believed supporting others in their grief needed to be a grand gesture of some sort—a homemade meal or a large bouquet of flowers. Because of my misled belief, I often resorted to either doing nothing at all if I couldn't find the time to "really show up" as I thought I should, or sending a donation of some kind to a fund if one was created.

On this side of grief, I now know that the small gestures that cost nothing are the ones that mean the most. It was the friend on the way to visit her son in college that told her husband to turn the car around and come back to the hospital to be with me when my mother had been diagnosed, and I didn't know what to do. It was the phone calls late into the evening from friends and family, where only sobs and whimpers were heard on either end, but we were together. It was the simple text, sent by a friend that read: "I'm thinking of you today and praying for you." And then, each year after she died, those who remembered the important days and thought to reach out to remind me that they, too, remembered my pain and shared in it.

In this comfort from others I have learned how to go forward in life and do for others what was done for me—or what I wish was done. Perhaps, for you, too, there are moments you can reflect on and see how you were given a moment of peace, passed on to you because of someone else's previous pain.

This isn't a comfort competition to try and outdo one another in gesture or sentiment. It is simply a calling placed on our lives now that we know grief and comfort in a new way. We can take this knowledge forward to bless others.

Knowing They Are Waiting

Perhaps one of the most important things my mother said to me in the letter she left was that when my time came to join her in heaven, she would meet me at the gates with her arms wide open. The image of my mother waiting to welcome me to my eternal home in heaven has sustained me through my deepest grief. During one particularly tearful phone call, I remember the determination in her voice cutting through my sorrow when she said, "Remember these words, we *will* see each other again."

And I have. I have remembered those words when the days and years without her here have felt too long, too difficult, and often too lonely. I *will* see her again. You *will* see your parent again.

After Mom died, I devoured books about near-death experiences. I wanted to know what she experienced in some way. I wanted proof that heaven was as real as I believed it to be.

In what can only be described as a wink from my mother and God, I applied for a freelance writing position with a Christian publication without knowing the topic matter.

"How do you feel about near-death experiences?" the editor asked.

"I've done nothing but read them the last six months and I am so intrigued by them," I said. This led to me spending the following year interviewing individuals who walked the line between life and death, and lived to share about a very real God, the indescribable love of Christ, and heaven.

Each conversation seemed to draw me closer to the heart of God, and I was left breathless by the passion each person had for sharing their story with as many people as they could. This life is only a *shadow* of the next. Each person who briefly visited heaven spoke of a place that was far more real than earth. I heard them try to put into words the beauty they experienced, and the overwhelming love they felt emanating from God, and eventually say that words could not do heaven justice. Their words gave me hope when I needed it most.

When we get to heaven, our parents will be there waiting. Quantrilla Ard looks forward to everything about heaven, but especially seeing her mother again. "I can't imagine what that moment is going to be like when we are reunited. I have a feeling I'll say, 'Lord, I love you, I really love you, but where's my mom?'"

Sophie Hudson also feels her mother may be waiting to greet her. "I think when we get to the end of our lives, maybe our parents will be the very ones to welcome us into that next chapter. If that's an option, I'm one hundred percent sure my mama will participate in that. That was her favorite thing, to welcome people into something new. The possibility is just really sweet to me, that when I get to the point of moving into the eternal part of my life, that she'll be there to greet me."

Life is short, yes. And we know in an intimate way now that heaven is only a breath and a pulse away from being a reality for each of us. We have experienced a loss that rocked us to our very core, and we do not grieve without hope. Your parent is as alive now as they ever were. But now they wait beyond a thin veil that will one day be removed.

Life is simple and complex, bitter and sweet, and everything in between—but it is so gloriously beautiful when we live it surrendered to the very love that has conquered death. Love never, ever dies. Let's show the world, and one another, now, with our beautifully broken hearts that love is eternal.

A Moment for Mindfulness

Finding a little time each day to consciously remember your parent is one way to process your feelings as time goes on, according to Clinical Psychologist Barbara Greenberg, PhD. "People may forget that you still need to talk about it after a while, and you may need permission to do so with others. If there were complicated feelings about your parent, you have to deal with them. You need to talk about the complicated feelings and add pieces to the narrative of this story so that it doesn't begin disrupting your sleep, because it does begin to sneak up on you in unexpected ways. You can write it all down or have pretend conversations with them. You need to get the feelings off your chest. If you take the time to consciously think of them a few minutes each day, the anniversaries won't hit you as hard. We don't flip the script on grief, though—any way you look at it—it's sad."

Greenberg, who recently experienced the loss of her brother, says creating something beautiful in his memory, such as a living memorial garden, helped her immensely. "We wanted to have something that would physically live on after his death. Planning the garden helped with the grieving process. If you have the means to plant something—even a plant inside your home—the action can be meaningful. In Israel, you plant a tree in memory of someone. In these ways, we have to honor what works for everyone in their grief."

Consider:

- Do you feel you need permission to speak about your parent or the experience of their illness now that some time has passed?
- Who are the people you feel safe to share with, even if the grief is no longer fresh?
- What feels like the best way to honor your parent?

JEN BABAKHAN

A Daughter's Prayer

Father, this road feels like a very long one I have been asked to travel without my parent. Help me to spend my time here without them in a way that honors You and their life, as well as the love we share still, even now that they are home with You. Bring to my mind those You would have me comfort in the way I have been comforted and guide me to know how to show them Your love in their time of pain. Remind me of Your presence when I yearn for all I've lost and give me a heart of gratitude for all I've been given. Amen.

CLOSING THOUGHTS

When you come to the end of this long road, your mother or father is still yours. Neither time nor grief can take them from you—where they live forever in heart and mind. Somewhat surprisingly, grief may become a way you still feel close to them, something you cherish instead of aim to lose. It isn't wallowing to continue to grieve—it is wise acceptance. For all their mistakes and missteps, quirks and endearing qualities, your parent was and is *yours*—forever.

It has been an honor to walk this sacred journey with you. I pray that among these pages you found the comfort and encouragement you needed, exactly when you needed it. I hope that when you look in the mirror, you see the strength you have gained more than the exhaustion you have felt.

The woman in front of you has been through some things, and she's survived. She's equipped now with more empathy than when she began. She knows grief, not as something to fear, but as a friend who guides her gently into peace.

She knows that life is uncertain. We cannot know the future—and she wouldn't have it any other way. She has moments tucked into her heart that she knows were gifts from God.

Her faith has been built through fire, and the heat has forged an enduring connection to her Creator. She walks in confidence that there is always more: more hope, more faith, more peace, and above all, more love.

You are different now. You are not who you were. You are forever changed. A new life awaits you now, as much as it awaited your parent upon his or her arrival to eternity. I pray you walk into it with deep peace.

More than anything, my hope as you close this book, is that you know you never walk alone—not in this life, and not in the next.

NOTES

1. Chapter 5: Anticipating the Impossible. Meghan O'Rourke, *Story's End* (*The New Yorker*, March 7, 2011)
2. Chapter 9: Walking Through Broken Glass. Shel Silverstein, *Every Thing On It* (New York: HarperCollins, 2011), 22

ACKNOWLEDGMENTS

This book took me on a journey into some of my most deeply felt moments of sorrow and joy. I am immensely grateful to those who supported me along this path. My deepest gratitude to:

My husband, Ed, and our precious boys, Bryce and Bradley—Thank you for giving me the space and time to do this emotionally difficult work while encouraging me to keep going when I wanted to quit. I love you more than words can express.

My father, Larry Nyquist—There is no handbook for losing a soulmate, but you have taught us all how to grieve and live with grace. You love us so well, and your example teaches us daily. Mom is so proud. I love you.

Zach and Berenice Nyquist—Thank you for your support throughout everything, I don't know what I would have done without you both. And thank you for the cutest nephew on earth. I love you all dearly.

Nikki Echabarne—Your consistent encouragement and prayers held me steady on this path. I'm so grateful. Love you, sweet friend.

Quantrilla Ard, Mary Boswell, Sophie Hudson, Becky Keife, Shay Mason, Becky McCoy, and Jaime Jo Wright—Your willingness to be vulnerable and allow me the great honor of sharing your experiences on these pages is a privilege I am deeply grateful for. I pray this book honors the memory of your precious parent.

Barbara Greenberg, PhD; Sherry Lewis; and Nicole Zasowski—Your incredible wisdom added meaningful depth to each chapter. Thank you for the tremendous gift of your time and talent. I am so honored to know each of you.

My literary agent, Debbie Alsdorf—From the moment we met, you were a source of deep spirit-led encouragement, and I am grateful to know you. Thank you for believing in me and this project from the start. You are a gift.

To Jesus, my Savior and truest friend—There are no words to express the way You have carried me in the deepest valleys. I'll spend my eternity thanking You.

www.ingramcontent.com/pod-product-compliance
Lightning Source LLC
Chambersburg PA
CBHW022110090426
42743CB00008B/790